SWITCHED ON POP

Switched On Pop

*How Popular Music Works,
and Why It Matters*

Nate Sloan
AND Charlie Harding
ILLUSTRATIONS BY Iris Gottlieb

OXFORD
UNIVERSITY PRESS

OXFORD
UNIVERSITY PRESS

Oxford University Press is a department of the University of Oxford. It furthers
the University's objective of excellence in research, scholarship, and education
by publishing worldwide. Oxford is a registered trade mark of Oxford University
Press in the UK and certain other countries.

Published in the United States of America by Oxford University Press
198 Madison Avenue, New York, NY 10016, United States of America.

Library of Congress Cataloging-in-Publication Data
Names: Sloan, Nate, 1986– author. | Harding, Charlie, 1986– author. |
Gottlieb, Iris, illustrator.
Title: Switched on pop : how popular music works & why it matters /
Nate Sloan & Charlie Harding ; illustration by Iris Gottlieb.
Description: New York, NY : Oxford University Press, [2020] |
Includes bibliographical references and index.
Identifiers: LCCN 2019007775| ISBN 9780190056650 (hardcover : alk. paper) |
ISBN 9780190056674 (epub)
Subjects: LCSH: Popular music—2001–2010—History and criticism. |
Popular music—2011–2020—History and criticism. |
Popular music—Analysis, appreciation.
Classification: LCC ML3470 .S6 2020 | DDC 781.64—dc23
LC record available at https://lccn.loc.gov/2019007775

9 8 7 6 5 4 3 2

Printed by LSC Communications, United States of America

The *Switched on Pop* logo is a copyright (2020) of Rock Ridge Productions, LLC,
designed by Courtney Leonard and Vox Media.

All time markers refer to the version of each song included in the accompanying
Spotify playlist, https://spoti.fi/31ZZmYK. Listed dates for each song reflect when
it was first released in the U.S.

For Whitney and Bess

Contents

SWITCHED ON POP

Introduction

Switched On Pop

Carly Rae Jepsen—"Call Me Maybe"

HEY I JUST MET YOU.   AND THIS IS CRAZY,   BUT HERE'S MY NUMBER   SO CALL ME MAYBE

How perfect are those lines? They feel as old as the earth, like something archaeologists would discover carved in stone at an ancient Druid burial ground. But of course it's not just the words that resonate; it's the music that is subconsciously added to them by anyone who has heard Carly Rae Jepsen's 2012 #1 hit "Call Me Maybe." It's the rhythm, melody, and harmony of the line that make the lyric so effective. The music thrusts listeners into the position of the song's narrator, into the state of suspended animation that comes from doing one of the bravest and scariest things in the world: asking someone out. The preceding verse finds Jepsen in a more contemplative mood, narrating her interior emotions. But in the chorus, Jepsen—and her listeners— suddenly plunge into real time. Through four lines, over four measures of music, Jepsen and her co-writers Tavish Crowe and Josh Ramsay generate heart-pounding suspense. Jepsen delivers her first lyric, "Hey, I just met you." Then, she pauses, as

"Call Me Maybe" performed by Carly Rae Jepsen, written by Jepsen, Josh Ramsay, Tavish Crowe, Schoolboy Records, 2012.

if waiting for a response, but there is none. The silence isn't filled by another voice, only by synthesized strings sounding out the syncopated rhythm "daa da da." Inconclusive, at best. How will the object of her affection respond? Jepsen continues, "And this is crazy." Another pause, another syncopated string stab. "But here's my number." Another string hit. "So call me, maybe?"

Every other musical element in the chorus reinforces the exquisite awkwardness of the encounter between Jepsen and her crush. Nervous about showing her feelings, Jepsen hesitates before singing the first word of the chorus, "hey." The lyric is probably better written as "[pause] hey." One might expect Jepsen to sound the word on the downbeat, the first pulse of a musical measure. Instead, she waits until the second beat. It's unexpected, but effective, like she's working up the courage to say her piece. The chorus's underlying chord progression also keeps things up in the air. The progression never lands on what we call the tonic chord, in this case, G major, the harmonic "home" of the song. It only glances at it. In fact, the only time that the harmony firmly lands on G major is on the very last chord of the song—an absence that makes listeners feel giddily unmoored.

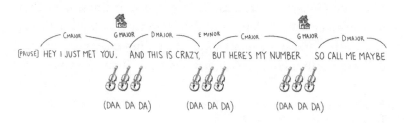

This avoidance-of-the-home-chord technique in "Call Me Maybe" is similar to one used in Katy Perry's "Teenage Dream" (2010). In a 2014 article for Slate, the musician Owen Pallett describes how the lack of a home chord in Perry's hit creates "suspension . . . in the emotional sense, which listeners often associate with 'exhilaration,' being on the road, being on a roller coaster, travel." In 2014, Nate and Charlie were traveling down the California coast with their partners Whitney and Bess. Nate and Charlie were sharing the backseat, where they were often banished in order to quarantine their music geekery from innocent bystanders such as their spouses. Both had read Owen's piece on "Teenage Dream" and were aflame with new respect for the musical integrity that animates even the bubbliest of bubblegum pop. Nate had been teaching high school students about music theory and was sharing with Charlie the insights the class had gleaned from their analysis of "Call Me Maybe." The closer one listened to the song, it seemed, the more one could uncover. It may be commercial fluff, but the artistry behind the fluff was undeniable.

The moment was revelatory. Until then, Nate and Charlie had been, well, snobs. Charlie was more of a rock/electronic snob, after a childhood of learning how to shred on guitar and a postcollegiate affair with trancey, late-night synthesizer sessions. Nate leaned more toward jazz/classical snobbery, having studied jazz piano in high school and then discovering the joys of obscure, atonal music in college. Charlie became a songwriter with a day job and Nate got a PhD in historical musicology. Still, pop represented the final frontier, the forbidden pleasure. And when we, Nate and Charlie, broke down the walls and let pop into our lives, everything changed. Not just our relationship with pop but our relationship with the world. It turned out that the only thing preventing us from enjoying pop was our own bias against it.

We wanted to share this epiphany, so we started a podcast and called it *Switched On Pop* after Wendy Carlos's innovative album *Switched On Bach* (1968), which recreated classical music with electronic instruments to demonstrate that a synthesizer could convey as much beauty and depth as a cello. Following Carlos's lead, we aimed to illuminate the musical integrity of pop songs. This was in the early days of the second podcast boom, when the runaway success of *Serial* launched the medium into the collective conscious and presented the perfect vehicle for *Switched On Pop*: on a podcast audiences could actually *hear* the musical examples we wanted to describe. With Carly Rae watching over us, we were off. Astonishingly, people wanted to listen. The show's audience grew steadily. As it did, people stopped wanting just to listen—they wanted to talk, to ask questions. To write ten-page emails alleging that the sonority of the third chord in One Direction's latest track proved that two of its members were in a secret romance.

We couldn't get enough. Our ambition expanded. We brought on performers, critics, songwriters, technologists—anyone with an interesting story to tell about the *music* of pop. Soon, we were far from alone in the quest to listen deeply to pop. We write this in a golden age of popular music analysis. Podcasts like *Dissect, Song Exploder,* and *Twenty Thousand Hertz* examine music on levels that border on the molecular. Online publications such as *Slate* and *Vox* expound on trends in pop composition, while the *Earworm* web video series historicizes modern pop sounds. In the academy, pop has gained traction as a valuable site of study. Still, though we live in a golden age of popular music theory, there's a dearth of texts that offer ways to understand the sonic world of pop. Podcast listeners regularly write us asking where they can find such a tome, and we have nothing to offer. Until now.

Switched On Pop contains sixteen studies of pop hits from 2000 to 2019. Each chapter homes in on a single musical property that acts as a lens for examining how and why the song in question is so successful. Each chapter is self-contained, but the ideas in them are portable and can be applied to a range of music, both popular and beyond.

Picking sixteen songs to represent twenty years of popular music presented a challenge. There simply was no way to represent the full richness and complexity of twenty-first-century pop in a single book. Our method was to select songs that, first of all, are extremely popular. Beyond that, we selected songs that we love, and ones that we believe will last. We cast for songs belonging strictly to pop as well those from wider popular music genres like country, electronic dance music (EDM), and hip hop in order to probe the borders of the pop sound. Finally, we chose songs that scaffold essential musical knowledge, with each chapter informing the next. The first six chapters offer a crash course in the building blocks of music: rhythm in Outkast; melody in Taylor Swift; harmony in Fun; form in Rihanna; timbre in Sia; and lyric in Justin Timberlake. The next seven chapters dig deeper into the sound of pop: the hook in Ariana Grande; rhyme in Drake; syncopation in Kendrick Lamar; key changes in Beyoncé; counterpoint in Britney Spears; sampling in M.I.A.; and sound design in Skrillex. The final three chapters illuminate some of the more formidable elements of popular music in the new millenium: tonal ambiguity in Luis Fonsi; genre in Kelly Clarkson; and musical identity as presented by Kanye West, Jay Z, and Toby Keith.

We believe that we can better appreciate the role that popular music plays in our lives by focusing on how its music works. Sometimes, music operates according to age-old properties that can be found in the work of classical composers like Bach and Beethoven. Other times, pop creates its own rules, pushes against received compositional wisdom, and points toward new musical possibilities. By examining the artistry of stars like Beyoncé, Sia, and Skrillex, we see that their place in the pop pantheon is owed not just to their celebrity but also to their musicality—whether refined through study or channeled through instinct.

Like so much pop, the creation of "Call Me Maybe" does not map to the genius myth common to high art. Carly Rae Jepsen did not stand on an oceanside cliff, lift her brow skyward, and wait for divine inspiration to bellow, "Hey, I just met you." "Call Me Maybe" thus raises a question that listeners of our podcast ask over and over: do these musicians even know what they're doing? That is, did Jepsen and her collaborators sit down and consciously decide to avoid using the tonic chord until the end of the song in order to increase the harmonic tension? Are these musical choices even intentional? The answer is, sometimes. Max Martin, the Swedish mastermind behind more hits in the twenty-first century than anyone else, is known to approach a song with panoptic precision, an approach that has been dubbed "melodic math." On the other hand, songwriter Emily Warren told us in an interview on *Switched On Pop* that she's never started a song with such calculation but rather proceeds completely by intuition. When a producer working with Sia complained that she made the same amount of money for writing a song in twenty minutes that would take him three weeks to produce, Sia replied, "Yeah . . . but it took me fifteen years to take twenty minutes." "Call Me Maybe" is likely a song built from a mix of clever engineering and happy accidents. The song began life as a country tune before its writers realized that the pop textures most listeners are now familiar with would prove more effective. Some lyrics don't really make any sense, like "Before you came into my life I missed you so bad." And yet, it doesn't seem to matter, because the line's rhythm and melody are so expertly crafted.

Every type of music lover has something to learn from listening to pop. It is not essential to love every song in this book, but it is essential to take them all seriously—which is not always easy to do. Critics often dismiss pop music as corporate, a Marxist's nightmare of boorish middle-aged svengalis presiding over an assembly line of aural baubles destined for the brainwashed masses. There is truth in the image. There is a lot of bad music, and there are plenty of terrible musicians out there. There are also genuine artists among the bunch, and that is who we have sought to represent in these pages. And even when pop is the product of corporate strategy sessions and focus groups, its music remains unruly. It does not obey the intentions of its creators. As manicured or messy as a song may be, once it's released into the world, predicting how it will resonate is impossible. Listeners take music and remake it in their own image. As the cultural theorist Stuart Hall has noted, there are two ways to read the term "popular." One is popular as the product of mass media. Oppressive, reductive, prizing commercial success over artistic integrity. The other is popular as in "of the people," accessible art that soothes the pain of everyday life. Hall concludes that popular art is never one or the other, solely top-down or bottom-up, but rather a negotiation, a dialogue, a give-and-take between the two.

"Call Me Maybe" is a perfect example of the deeply collaborative and commercial nature of twenty-first-century pop, and in this respect, the art and business of making pop music has changed little since the invention of the phonograph in the late 1800s. At the same time, the twenty-first century presents new iterations of certain themes. Popular music reflects the society, economy, and technology of the world from which it emerges, so by learning the language of pop we can better understand our mad, modern existence. To be switched on is to be curious about how every part of a song interweaves to create movement and meaning. When we listen this way, we find that the injustice, inequality, and intolerance of the world is all in there, but so is its beauty, kindness, and wonder. If, as Stuart Hall suggests, popular culture is a dialogue, then when we listen more clearly, we engage more clearly too. Switched on listening will help you better enjoy the songs you love, better appreciate the songs you don't, make you a more politically engaged and socially empathetic listener, help you relate to your fellow citizens, and embrace change. Also—and this is crazy—it's absurdly fun.

1

Y'all Don't Want to Hear Me, You Just Want to Dance

Meter: Outkast—"Hey Ya!"

In the beginning, there was the beat. The maternal heartbeat is the first sound heard in the womb. Although many elements of music are tightly intertwined—rhythm, melody, harmony, timbre, and form—our prenatal relationship to rhythm makes it an ideal place to begin a journey to the heart of pop music. And few songs testify to the power of rhythm better than André Benjamin's masterpiece of shifting temporality, "Hey Ya!" (2003). The infectious funk underlying this ode to shaking it "like a Polaroid picture" pulls attention from the heartbreaking lyrics, which question whether a lasting relationship is truly possible. Benjamin himself anticipated this distraction from the song's message, singing "Y'all don't want to hear me, you just want to dance." Despite its existential melancholy, "Hey Ya!" topped the charts, went platinum, and effectively brought the Polaroid camera back to life. Why does "Hey Ya!" remain such a dance floor staple almost two decades after its release? The answer in part lies in a device employed by the artist once known as André 3000

"Hey Ya!" performed by Outkast, written by André Benjamin, LaFace Records, 2003.

in which he alters the beat for one measure in every chorus. This effect, what musicians call "mixed meter," delights and unsettles at once, and understanding it is key to understanding the funky subversion of "Hey Ya!"

In order to hear how this Outkast hit upsets our perception of musical time, it's first necessary to define a few rhythmic concepts: beat, pulse, tempo, and meter. Like many musical terms, **beat** has a few meanings. It can refer to a repeating drum pattern, as in Taylor Swift's exhortation toward the end of "Shake It Off" (2014) that listeners, instead of worrying about "all the liars and cheats," should be "getting down to this sick beat." In hip hop, beat can also refer to the entire instrumental backing track of a song, like the late Lil Peep's lyric on "Star Shopping" (2015): "Shout out to everyone makin' my beats, you helpin' me preach." The purest form of beat, though, relates to **pulse**, steady rhythmic repetition at a constant interval. Like the pumping of blood through the veins, pulse is a universal phenomenon.

Our heartbeat primes us as humans to perceive rhythmic repetition, and we are instinctively drawn to any steady, repeated beat. We often find ourselves nodding along to the clicking car blinker while waiting for a turn, tapping our foot in time to a clopping horse, or snapping our fingers to the rhythms emitted from a deskjet printer. The power of pulse is clear from the first moment of "Hey Ya!," when Benjamin shouts "1, 2, 3, *unh!*"—four evenly spaced beats that plunge the listener into the song. After Benjamin establishes the pulse in his count off, it recedes to the background and it is not sounded by any instrument. Yet we continue to tap our feet and feel the beat. Sometimes identifying a song's underlying pulse can be hard because the beat is inaudible. Often it is absent but implied, like the grid that lies underneath a Michelangelo fresco, giving the scene order but long painted over. In other songs, the pulse is unavoidable: "The Chain" (1977), by Fleetwood Mac, features drummer Mick Fleetwood pounding out every single beat on his bass drum, a musical corollary to the song's cry to "never break the chain."

Another question comes up when dealing with pulse: how fast is it? The answer lies in **tempo**, the speed at which music is played, or the rate of its pulse. Tempo can be measured in beats per minute (BPM). A fast tempo will have a higher BPM and a slower one will have a lower BPM. Humans have upper and lower limits to the tempo that we can process: nothing higher than 300 or lower than 40 BPM. In between lies a "sweet spot." From the 1940s to the 2010s, the average tempo of Top 40 pop has remained right around 120 BPM. This particular rate strikes a remarkable correlation with what physiologists identify as the human body's "preferred tempo." As humans like to listen to music with a tempo of 120 BPM, they also like to walk at about 120 steps per minute (New Yorkers excepted). Cardiopulmonary resuscitation (CPR), meanwhile, needs to be administered at around 100 BPM—which is why doctors recommend using the Bee Gees track "Stayin' Alive" (103 BPM) as a guide. The 160 BPM tempo of "Hey Ya!" would be much too fast for performing CPR, but the quick tempo is essential for the unceasing energy Benjamin generates over the course of the track.

Returning to the intro of "Hey Ya!," something else happens as Benjamin shouts "1, 2, 3, *unh!*" Not only does he establish a pulse and a tempo, he establishes **meter**—grouping beats together into a recognizable unit. If we imagine a pulse as a series of evenly spaced beats, each represented by Benjamin's visage, its simplest expression would look like Figure 1.1.

It looks like a perfectly effective pulse, but also a somewhat boring one—just an undifferentiated, infinite stream of identical beats. An easy way to spice it up is to divide the beats into groups. Taking a cue from Benjamin's four-beat count off, let us group our beats in sets of four. We can illustrate this by simply

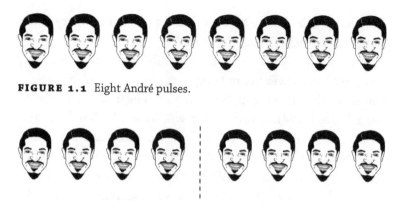

FIGURE 1.1 Eight André pulses.

FIGURE 1.2 Two measures of four André pulses.

adding bar lines after each grouping of Benjamin-heads, measuring out four each time (Figure 1.2).

This "measuring out" of beats is why any group of them,
measured out and separated by a barline, is called a **measure** or
a **bar**, and the reason why this larger system of measuring out
beats is called meter.

Grouping together four Benjamin-beats has gone a long way
toward imposing some kind of repeatable meter onto the infinite
stream, but the bar lines and measures we created above cannot
be heard; they're just visual markers. We need something that
will aurally delineate our chosen grouping. One solution is to dif-
ferentiate the first pulse, or **downbeat**, of each of our measures
by accenting it—giving it a little more *oomph* than the others.
Visually, we can illustrate this by giving each Benjamin-downbeat
a fez (Figure 1.3).

Now we have turned infinite pulse into ordered meter, which
in turn gives a sense of symmetry and progression that grabs
both the mind and body, moving them to dance. Not that every
song has pulse and meter. Plenty of music, especially religious
music like Quranic recitation, Jewish cantillation, and Gregorian

FIGURE 1.3 Two measures of four André pulses with downbeat accents.

chant, creates a state of hypnotic flow by avoiding any sense of steady pulse. In many of these traditions, the aim is to focus on the holy words being pronounced, and a perceptible beat might distract from that attentive mode. The lack of pulse is a significant part of why religious musical traditions are such powerful vehicles for spiritual meditation and contemplation. In the world of pop music, though, every song has a beat. Pulse encourages bodily movement, which is a key feature of pop. Beat is the reason it's easy to boogie to Beyoncé but hard to get down to Gregorian chant.

As humans display a preferred tempo for pop music at around 120 BPM, they also show a preference for four-beat meters. This was not always the case, however. Around the turn of the twentieth century a sea change took place that we might dub "The Great Metric Shift." Prior to 1900, most popular songs used meters that measured beats into groups of three, the same meter one would find in a waltz. From hits like "After the Ball" (1891) by Charles K. Harris, the first song to go platinum by selling two million copies of sheet music, to "Take Me Out to the Ballgame" (1908), by Jack Norworth and Albert von Tilzer, three-beat waltz meter reigned supreme. That all changed during the first decades of the twentieth century, through a musical style pioneered by black musicians called ragtime. With its two-beat meter and ragged-edged syncopations, ragtime played against the traditional three-beat waltz and, by extension, against customary Victorian sensibilities. As the decades progressed, jazz musicians expanded ragtime's two-beat meter into a four-beat meter, which became the default meter of popular music. Today, ragtime sounds like a quaint, old-timey style of music that speaks to a simpler era. In its day, though, ragtime rocked American culture to its core and elicited the same anxious reactions that would later meet jazz, rock, and hip hop.

That each of these musical styles originated with and were practiced by black musicians speaks to the latent racial fears that underlie many "objective" aesthetic critiques of musical innovations. In 1900, one music magazine writing about ragtime complained that "the counters of the music stores are loaded with this virulent poison which in the form of a malarious [sic] epidemic, is finding its way into the homes and brains of the youth to such an extent as to arouse one's suspicions of their sanity." The same language of race and pathology would bubble up in 1928 when the writer Maxim Gorky criticized jazz as made up of "an orchestra of madmen, sexual maniacs," or in 1992 when presidential candidate George H. W. Bush called the music of rap group N.W.A. "sick." The line between hot rhythm and racism has always been thin.

André Benjamin's four-beat "1, 2, 3, *unh!*" count-off in "Hey Ya!" sounds natural to our modern ears, but it is the product of decades of metric upheaval. Today the relative absence of three-beat meters suggests that we are still very much living in an age shaped by the rhythmic vision of African American musical practice. A defining moment in the Great Metric Shift might be Marvin Gaye's performance of "The Star-Spangled Banner" at the 1983 NBA All-Star Game. The national anthem was created when someone took a poem by Francis Scott Key and set the words to a British drinking song from the 1700s—one in a three-beat meter (Figure 1.4).

Marvin Gaye's soulful reinterpretation of the anthem did the unthinkable: it changed the song's original three-beat meter to a four-beat meter. This had only happened once before, when Jose

Feliciano sang the "Star-Spangled Banner" as a folk song at the 1968 baseball World Series and also turned the three-beat meter into four. One baseball fan called Feliciano's rendering "a disgrace, an insult." Gaye's metric revision did not garner the same controversy, and neither did it make a huge impression at the time. Eight years later, however, the impact of Gaye's metrical shift would be felt when Whitney Houston performed the national anthem at the 1991 Super Bowl. Inspired by Gaye, Houston's iconic rendition of the anthem also switched the meter to groups of four, and her incandescent performance set a new standard for all others to follow. Beyoncé followed in Houston's footsteps in 2013 at Barack Obama's inauguration, the final step in reimagining the anthem in a four-beat meter, as shaped by a Puerto Rican immigrant and three generations of African American singers. Unlike at Feliciano's performance, no one batted an eye when Beyoncé revised the anthem's time signature. By then, there was no question: our nation's heart beats in four-beat time (Figure 1.5).

At this point, we are equipped to discuss the basics of rhythm: beat, pulse, tempo, and meter. This is essential for breaking down "Hey Ya!" because in an unusual move, the Outkast track doesn't employ the same meter throughout. While we live in the age of the Great Metric Shift, and while André Benjamin kicks off "Hey Ya!" with a crystalline "1, 2, 3, *unh!*" four-count, the song is not entirely in four-beat meter. The closer you listen, the stranger the song appears. "Hey Ya!" begins predictably enough, with three measures of four-beat meter. This is easy to feel if you continue counting groups of four pulses following Benjamin's "1, 2, 3, *unh!*" count-off. The pattern repeats three times, but then the counts strangely stop lining up with the meter of the song, right on the words "know for" in the line "and this I know for sure." That's because a rogue measure of two beats, emerging seemingly from nowhere, interrupts the prevailing four-beat meter. As quickly as

FIGURE 1.4 The "Star Spangled Banner" in three-beat meter.

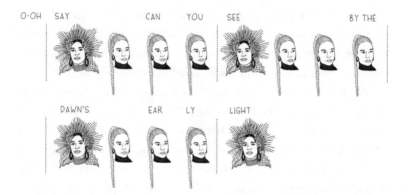

FIGURE 1.5 Beyoncé's "Star Spangled Banner" in four-beat meter.

it appears, the odd-man-out measure of two disappears, and the song moves back to four-beat meter on the word "sure." "Hey Ya!" continues this asymmetric pattern for the rest of the track: three measures of four-beat meter, a two-beat interruption, then back to four-beat meter for another two measures. Then the cycle repeats, surprising dancers with each injection of two-bar meter (Figure 1.6).

In 2014, Benjamin revealed a surprising fact while discussing the genesis of "Hey Ya!" with Ali Shaheed Muhammad, the Tribe Called Quest DJ and host of National Public Radio's hip hop show, *Microphone Check*: his use of mixed meter in his 2003 smash was directly inspired by Aretha Franklin's 1968 recording of the Burt Bacharach and Hal David composition "I Say a Little Prayer." If you're feeling bewildered as to the similarities between Benjamin's song about how "nothing is forever" and Franklin's song about how "forever and ever you'll stay in my heart," rest assured you are not alone. It's hard to hear because the similarity exists only on the level of meter. Both songs feature the same two-beat interruption, in exactly the same place. The metric similarity between "Hey Ya!" and "I Say a Little Prayer" becomes apparent if you place the two tracks side-by-side (Figure 1.7).

Inspired by Bacharach, who loves writing songs with unusual metric shifts and odd groupings of pulses, Benjamin turned "Hey Ya!" from a typical pop confection into a rare bird. Like Bacharach, Benjamin executes his metric shifts so that they often go unnoticed because his temporal play sounds so natural, so earned and right. Though rare, these two composers are not alone in indulging in changing meters. They represent nodes in a long tradition of rhythmic experiments that together make up an alternative canon of metric ambiguity.

Having broken down the mechanics of the metric bait-and-switch in "Hey Ya!," let's zoom out and consider the effect this rhythmic gambit has on the way people perceive the song. By any gauge, "Hey Ya!" is one of the biggest hits of the twenty-first century. In many ways, it is synonymous with larger cultural and economic changes of the new millennium. "Hey Ya!" helped launch the fledgling iTunes music service as the most downloaded song in the first year of the platform's existence. It would go on to become the first song to reach one million digital downloads and the first single whose digital sales outpaced its physical

FIGURE 1.6 "Hey Ya" with three measures of four, a measure of two, and a measure of four beats.

FIGURE 1.7 "Hey Ya" borrows its mixed meter from Aretha Franklin's "I Say a Little Prayer."

sales. Even as "Hey Ya!" rode the digital wave, it also kickstarted a trend of nostalgia that would mark each subsequent technological innovation. André Benjamin may have helped iTunes get off the ground, but he also almost single-handedly revived the fading fortunes of the Polaroid Corporation—although Polaroid did have to issue a public statement discouraging its users from shaking their developing photos for fear of damage.

"Hey Ya!" also foreshadowed the blurring of genre that would mark the sound of pop in the new millenium. Rappers like Kanye

West and Drake have since made singing a core element of their technique, but when Benjamin released "Hey Ya!" he was nervous about how it would be received: "I was completely terrified . . . because I'm coming from a rap world and everybody got they face frowned up and wanna be as tough as possible and you out there singing." Instead of drawing inspiration from hip hop, Benjamin looked to punk acts like the Ramones, the Buzzcocks, and the Smiths. He recorded every instrument save the bass synthesizer himself and composed the song using the first four chords he ever learned on guitar: G major, C major, D major, and E major. Despite the rapturous reception for "Hey Ya!," Benjamin found himself uneasy with its success, and he was musically aimless following its release. But eventually, his interest in musical experimentation returned in force. Fast-forward to 2018, and Benjamin's SoundCloud release, "Look Ma, No Hands," might represent the apex of his avant-garde approach: a seventeen-minute free improvisation on the bass clarinet indebted more to John Coltrane than to Atlanta hip hop.

"Look Ma" was far from a hit, garnering less than 30,000 plays on SoundCloud as of this writing. Beyond the track's length and meandering structure, the song has no definitive pulse or meter. As Benjamin foretold, it appears that "Y'all don't want to hear me, you just wanna dance." This lyric is the key to unlocking André's years in the artistic desert, and it might also help us interpret the meaning of the metric shift in "Hey Ya!" The enthusiasm of the music contradicts the sobriety of the lyrics, which focus on rejection, unhappiness, and the fallacy that love can last forever. In this respect, "Hey Ya!" is far from alone. Other pop songs have managed to pull the musical wool over audiences' ears. The photogenic brothers in Hanson had a monster hit in 1997 with the jaunty, infectious single "MMMBop." The song's bright harmonies and textures obscured its lyrics about the impermanence hiding beneath every relationship. Even its titular nonsense lyric points to how fast the deepest bond can break: "You turn your back," and "in an mmmbop they're gone." Bruce Springsteen's "Born in the U.S.A." (1984) has the sound of a nationalist anthem with its major harmonies, soaring vocals, and ringing drum hits. But a close listen to the lyrics reveals a searing critique of US domestic and foreign policy right from its first line, "Born down in a dead man's town." Despite the existential despair of its lyrics, candidates like Ronald Reagan, Bob Dole, Pat Buchanan, and Donald Trump have all used Springsteen's song in political rallies. "Pumped Up Kicks" (2010) by Foster the People is a bleak song about a school shooting, one of the only hits to have tackled such a difficult topic. Nevertheless, "Pumped Up Kicks" possesses such a catchy melody that the song has scored scenes in the television shows *Entourage* and *Gossip Girl*, and was even used as the soundtrack for an Australian beer commercial. Like these songs, "Hey Ya!" leads a double life. Benjamin's meditation on insecurity is today, according to Spotify, one of the ten most-played songs at weddings over the past decade. Playing "Hey Ya!" at your wedding is the romantic equivalent of playing "Born in the U.S.A." at a political rally, and yet, the inherent contradiction does not seem to register. Once again, "Y'all don't want to hear me, you just want to dance."

Still, the lie in Benjamin's song is right there under the surface. Even for those who don't want to hear and just want to dance, the metrical ground keeps shifting beneath their feet. Benjamin seems to be challenging listeners to look away. Like the dissonance between the music and the lyrics, the metric dissonance in "Hey Ya!" does nothing to impede the song's feverish pleasures. The mixed meter gets subsumed into the relentless groove of this millennial magnum opus. Which, of course, is exactly to the point. "Hey Ya!" is a song about denial that has listeners denying its musical truth every time they press play. Over and over, one thing is clear: "Y'all don't hear me, you just want to dance."

A Star's Melodic Signature

Melody: Taylor Swift—"You Belong with Me"

Taylor Swift is a musical chameleon who changes her style from album to album. Over the course of her career, each release has marked a musical departure from the last, charting a development from country ingenue, to crossover icon, to pop megastar. These drastic changes are part of the reason she is as scorned as she is beloved. To some critics and listeners, Swift seems fake, lacking an authentic, "true" personality and voice.

Of course, this is exactly what pop stars are supposed to do: perform identity. And what often gets lost amid all the drama surrounding Swift—the love, the hate, and the endless gossip—is her ingenious songwriting ability. Although each reinvention finds her scrubbing and rewriting her musical playbook, there are elements of Swift's songcraft that stay constant through each successive phase of her identity. In this way Swift is a bit like Pablo Picasso, who changed styles throughout his career like most of us change socks. You might never guess that the same artist painted the impressionist *Old Woman* in 1901, the cubist

"You Belong With Me" performed by Taylor Swift, written by Swift and Liz Rose, Big Machine Records, 2009.

Guitarist in 1911, and the neoclassical *Olga in an Armchair* in 1918. The only clue these works were painted by the same brush comes from the identical signature attached to each.

Musicians, though, cannot "sign" their songs. Unless, perhaps, they are DJ Mustard, who announces "Mustard on that beat!" as a sort of verbal signature on each track he produces, from YG to Rihanna—a forgery-resistant stamp for his original productions under constant siege from imitators. So even if Swift does not start each song with a cry of "Taylor on that melodic construction!" she and other songwriters can still leave their own melodic signatures within a song for forensic musicologists like ourselves to later exhume. Johann Sebastian Bach, for instance, developed his own personal "cryptogram," a four-note motif based on his name. In German Baroque music terminology, the letter "B" stands for the pitch "B-flat" and the letter "H" stands for the pitch "B." Thus, each letter of "Bach" can correspond to a single pitch: B-flat A, C, and B-natural. Johann Sebastian took advantage of the melody implied by his very name, dropping the four-note motif into a few compositions over the course of his career. Like Bach, Swift has her own melodic signature. Whether you are listening to a song like her anthem of unrequited teenage love, "You Belong with Me" (2009), the pop-country hybrid "Mean" (2010), or the alt-rock homage "State of Grace" (2012), you will find a common element present in each: a three-note melodic motif that we've termed the "T Drop."

To orient this particular melodic device, take a listen to "You Belong with Me." The first T Drop occurs at :59, toward the end of the song's chorus, when Swift sings the titular phrase "why can't you see/you belong with me?" On the word "see," Swift makes use of **melisma**, the practice of singing multiple pitches for a single syllable of text, turning the monosyllabic "see" into the tripartite "see-eee-eee." Melisma is a musical phenomenon that we will return to in Chapter 3, but for now let's focus on the three notes Swift sounds at this point in the song: B, A-sharp, and D-sharp. This pattern—descending a short distance, then descending a *big* drop—is one of the defining musical gestures of Swift's career, the secret signature stamped somewhere on every album she records.

Detecting Swift's melodic signature elsewhere in her oeuvre requires getting acquainted with the mysterious art of **melody.** Vocal timbre, the sound of an artist's voice (covered in Chapter 5), is the most immediate way that we can discern a pop star. Melodic construction makes for a more elusive marker of musical identity. Still, whether we are aware of it or not, melody is essential to the way we discern different artists—and even different musical traditions. At its most clinical, melody can be defined as a series of pitches laid out one-by-one in a distinct rhythmic profile. That's a straightforward explanation, but it certainly doesn't capture the *feeling* of getting caught up in melody, that mad rush of sensory pleasure that in 1919 moved songwriter Irving Berlin to insist "a pretty girl is like a melody/that haunts you night and day."

We will get to the source of Berlin's obsession, but before we can explain the haunting properties of melody we must wrap our heads around the concept of **pitch** and **scale**, because these are the building blocks from which melodies emerge. Let us start with pitch, which refers to the frequency at which a sound vibrates. Fast vibration translates to "high" pitches, slow vibrations to "low" pitches. Since frequency is just a rate of vibration, there are as many pitches as there are numbers—that is, infinite. Imagine sliding your finger along a violin string. Every small change in the point of contact between your finger and the string as you glide up or down would result in a *slightly* different pitch. Eventually in your wanton sliding, something notable would happen—you would reach a pitch that vibrates at a rate exactly twice as fast or slow as that of the pitch you started on. The distance between a given pitch and the one that vibrates twice as fast or slow is called an **octave**, and it has been used as the central unit for organizing pitch space going back to Ancient Greece. We can imagine pitch as a staircase, with each flight an octave —walk from the first step up to the landing twelve steps higher, and you've gone up one octave (Figure 2.1).

Pitches an octave apart express exactly the same kind of sonic quality, but they sound relatively higher or lower in terms of the overall frequency range. Taylor Swift jumps up an octave in "I Knew You Were Trouble" (2012), immediately following the end of the chorus at 1:05, right after she sings the line "now I'm lying on the cold, hard ground." When she moves from the word "ground" to the next word, "oh," she leaps from a low E-flat to

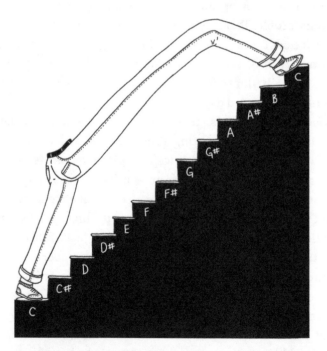

FIGURE 2.1 Scales are divided into equally spaced steps; each flight of twelve steps is one octave.

an E-flat exactly an octave higher. It's an exciting moment since an ascending octave leap is a difficult interval to land, as anyone who's tried singing Harold Arlen and Yip Harburg's "Somewhere Over the Rainbow" (1939), which *begins* with an ascending octave leap right on the word "some-where," can attest.

The octave thus became a crucial way of imposing order on the infinitude of pitch, infinite pitches being a fun idea in theory but presenting a problem in practice, one that the composer Igor Stravinsky referred to as the "abyss of freedom." Luckily for Igor, the Chinese musicologist Zhu Zaiyu calculated a way of dividing the octave back in 1584, breaking it down to a set of evenly spaced intervals. Think of this as the difference between a violin and guitar: the metal frets on a guitar organize the infinite possibilities of the violin string into a series of evenly divided spaces. We call Zhu Zaiyu's system *equal temperament*, and eventually most societies adopted the approach in various interpretations. Certain Arabic musical traditions chose to split the octave up into twenty-four tones, and to get a sense of the expanded pitch possibilities in this system you just have to imagine a piano with 176 keys instead of 88. The system that eventually won out around the globe, though, was Zhu Zaiyu's division of the octave into twelve evenly spaced tones. Still, once in a while a pop artist will sing pitches between the twelve standard ones. As the musician Jacob Collier has noted, Janelle Monáe does just that in her song "Make Me Feel" (2018) at :43, when she sings "I'm powerful, with a little bit of tender/An emotional, sexual bender." On "little bit of tender," and "sexual bender" Monáe dances between the twelve pitches of equal temperament.

There was much to be gained by agreeing to divide the octave into twelve tones using equal temperament, as different societies could describe and share music with greater precision. There was still an issue, however: how do you make sure one's instrument is in tune with another? Even as cultures across the world adopted equal temperament, there remained an unruly landscape of pitch standards. Different countries and cities would have wildly different notions of the rate at which a given pitch should vibrate. The difference could be as much as a half step or more between local standards—imagine the traveling professional musicians who had to adjust for every gig, and the soprano for whom the show-stopping high-C was suddenly a half step higher! Looking at it today, if a band wants to perform Swift's "Look What You Made Me Do" (2017) in the key of A minor, they need to ensure that all members of the band are using the same pitch frequency as a reference point. If the guitarist's definition of A vibrates at a different rate from the A of the bassist, then the performance will sound cacophonous no matter how neatly and evenly we all have agreed to divide up the octave.

The solution here was to assign one pitch a universal and unchanging frequency ratio that would be recognized around the world. From the early nineteenth century through to the mid-twentieth, there were numerous attempts at settling on a standard, generally around A4 = 435 Hz. In 1955, the slightly higher 440 Hz was affirmed by the International Organization for Standardization—and reaffirmed as recently as 1975. There remain some exceptions to this rule, notably so-called Historically Informed Performance practices of Baroque music that choose to make use of 415 Hz, one of the more common pitch standards of the German Baroque. But the advantage of having a universal standard is clear. Once everyone agrees to divide an octave into twelve equal tones using 440 Hz as a reference point, something unprecedented occurs: you can play middle C on a piano in Wichita, Kansas, and it will sound exactly the same as middle C on piano in Baku, Azerbaijan.

At this point, we are all pitched up and ready to go, except for one lingering issue. Pitches on their own are kind of boring. If you play up and down the twelve pitches that divide an octave in equal temperament, it just sounds like gobbledygook. Fear not, there is a musical device that will come to our rescue, take that mess of notes and turn them into something legible, nay, even pleasurable. Behold: the **scale**.

We know that anyone reading this who has taken music lessons at some point likely has a traumatic association with the word "scale." Nate's strict Russian piano teacher used to rap his knuckles with a rubber alligator if he failed to play his scales properly, and just hearing the word still elicits a painful Pavlovian response. Taylor Swift, who as a child would "play guitar until [her] fingers bled," can probably relate. But scales are actually our friends, or at the least, they are innocent bystanders in the music pedagogy wars. A scale is simply a collection of pitches that sound good together, drawn from the twelve evenly spaced tones that make up an octave.

Indeed, the particular ways that different cultures have chosen to order those twelve tones into specific scales is a big part of how we identify different musical styles. This is why the chorus of Jason Derulo's "Talk Dirty" (2013), for instance, sounds so exceptional in the landscape of Top 40 pop. The epic, honking sax line undergirding the song is sampled from the band Balkan Beat Box, and their melody in turn draws from a specific scale called the *Freygish*. This exotic-sounding scale is a distinct collection of pitches often used in Eastern European music, from funereal klezmer to Balkan party anthems. Derulo's track is thus as brilliant as it is outrageous. When Derulo sings, "Been around the world, don't speak the language/But your booty don't need explainin'," we are inclined to believe him, because just as he argues that booty is a universal language, so we can argue that we are all also melodic polyglots. We understand the *Freygish* scale in the song's sax sample, even if we have never heard it before, or at least not outside of a rousing round of "Hava Nagila" at a Bat Mitzvah.

In Ancient Greece, there were a number of different scales that used eight pitches to span the octave, many of which, centuries later, are still in use—just think of Maria and the Von Trapps singing "Do-Re-Mi-Fa-So-La-Ti-Do" in the *The Sound of Music* (1959). These eight-note scales are where we get the term octave, whose root "oct" means eight. Since the age of Pythagoras, two of the Greek scales have become prominent in modern pop: the **major scale** and the **minor scale**. The other common scale, the **pentatonic scale**, is much shorter, containing only five notes and also coming in a major and minor version. We hear the pentatonic scale in melodies ranging from "Pop Goes the Weasel," to "Amazing Grace," to Hall and Oates's "You Make My Dreams Come True" (1980) to Fetty Wap's "Trap Queen" (2015), to Swift's own "Delicate" (2017). Pretty much all of Swift's melodies are drawn from either the major, minor, or pentatonic scale.

Now that we have a sense of pitch and scale, let us return to melody. As we stated in the rather clinical definition above, melody is an arrangement of pitches, often drawn from a single scale, laid out one-by-one in a distinct rhythm. A melody does not have to use all of the notes of its source scale. In fact, there are multiple examples that use only a single pitch. French songs in the early 1900s used so many single-note melodies that one scholar calls them "more like Morse code than music." Antonio Carlos Jobim's self-referential *bossa nova* hit "Samba de Uma Nota Só" ("One Note Samba," 1960), follows the same maniacal focus on a single pitch. Swift herself uses this technique in a number of her songs, including in the chorus of "Out of the Woods" (2014) (Figure 2.2).

The chorus of Haim's rousing "I Want You Back" (2017) uses a grand total of two pitches. And the Chainsmokers' "Closer" (2016), a massive hit that ruled the Billboard charts for months, has a chorus that winds through the same three notes over and over, with an almost manic obsession. Melodies like this, that

FIGURE 2.2 A single-note melody in "Out of the Woods."

stick to pitches drawn from a single scale, are called **diatonic**. When songwriters use pitches that lie outside of the scale they have chosen it is called **chromaticism**—as in *chroma*, adding color to a melody by including pungent pitches that do not "belong" to the scale. Paul Simon, for one, is a big fan of this chromatic approach. In "Still Crazy after All These Years" (1975), he moves through all twelve pitches of the octave over the course of the song.

For the most part, though, pop melodies are diatonic in nature. In "You Belong with Me," for instance, there is not a single chromatic pitch. Given that there are so many diatonic melodies out there drawn from a seven-pitch scale, one might raise a question that has kept us up late many nights: *what if . . . someday . . . we run out of melodies??* This is not a ridiculous concern. If we take the twelve pitches of the equal temperament system and calculate every possible different melodic and rhythmic permutation, we end up with over one hundred quintillion possibilities. That is a number so high that your authors had to go look up what a "quintillion" is (it is a billion billions). That seems like an endless supply of melody! But, if we follow the Chainsmokers' example and focus on just *three* notes drawn from a scale, then the number of melodic possibilities tightens dramatically, down to only about 75,000 different combinations. That number seems concerning. Given that Drake releases approximately 10,000 songs a year, we should have run out of three-note melodies a decade ago.

And yet, the day of three-note "melody zero" has not arrived. Which brings us back, thankfully, to Taylor Swift. Making a powerful melodic gesture is not as easy as laying out a few pitches back-to-back. It is the art of arranging just the right pitch pattern, in just the right rhythm, paired with just the right lyrics, against just the right instrumental texture, sung with just the right vocal timbre. The songwriters who possess this alchemical gift are the ones we remember.

Part of the reason we respond to certain artists is because they have found a unique way of doing something with scales we know so well, sounding one of those 75,000 permutations in a way we have never heard before. In this way, artists like Swift develop their own melodic language, exemplified by the three-note motif of the T Drop. We can now return to "You Belong with Me," one of our favorite songs in Swift's catalog, and a track we place in the pop firmament alongside Jepsen's "Call Me Maybe" (2012), Prince's "Kiss" (1984), and Silver and Cohn's "Yes! We Have No Bananas" (1923).

"You Belong with Me" might be the song that crystallizes everything people love, and hate, about Swift's identity performance. It tells the story of a girl who is friend-zoned by the person she loves. She wants something more, but the object of her affection has no idea. This narrative is instantly relatable, and a huge part of Swift's success is her ability to tap into such universal scenarios. In this context, the T Drop on "see-ee-ee" creates in our ears a certain kind of sad resignation, a lachrymose descent that magnifies the tragedy of her unanswered question, "why can't you see?" (Figure 2.3). In "Mean," Swift's bittersweet song about bullying, the T Drop occurs at the end of a bridge

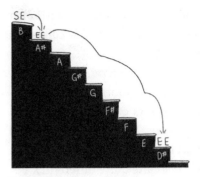

FIGURE 2.3 Taylor Swift's melodic "T Drop" signature descends a short distance then takes a big leap.

FIGURE 2.4 The "T Drop" in "Mean."

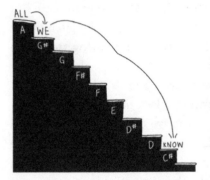

FIGURE 2.5 The "T Drop" in "State of Grace."

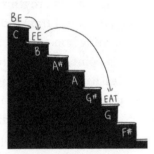

FIGURE 2.6 A "T Drop" variation in "Welcome to New York."

section in which the narrator imagines her tormentor's future: "I can see you years from now . . . drunk and grumbling on about how I can't sing." Right on the words "I can't sing," Swift sounds another T Drop, a melodic fall that captures the sad cycle of bullying (Figure 2.4).

When Swift uses the same motif in "State of Grace" (2012) at :44 under the lyrics "all we know/is touch and go," it conveys a similar sense of resignation (Figure 2.5).

The T Drop may serve as Swift's sonic signature, but the inherent plasticity of melody means that the motif signifies differently depending on small variations in its construction, as well as the overall context in which appears. The above examples all use the T Drop to convey a certain lyrical melancholy, but small changes to the motif can make it resonate quite differently. For instance, Swift uses a variation of the T Drop in "Welcome to New York" (2014) at 1:04 when she sings "I could dance to this beat." On the word "beat," Swift creates a melisma similar to the one on "see" in "You Belong with Me," stretching out the monosyllabic "beat" into a three-syllable "be-ee-eat" (Figure 2.6). But by changing both the rhythm of the T Drop and the pitch of the final note, the motif transforms from communicating sadness to communicating hope.

At this point, if readers find Taylor Swift's reliance on the T Drop excessive, perhaps indicating a lack of imagination or resourcefulness, it may prove instructive to compare her style to that of another great melodist, namely, Josquin des Prez, the Renaissance master who composed for the Sistine Chapel choir in the early sixteenth century. Take the distinctive four-note motif that kicks off Josquin's *Missa Pange lingua* (c. 1515). Josquin used this melodic combination a total of 704 times across 164 works, an amount that puts Swift's use of the T Drop to shame. Many songwriters use a sonic signature, whether intentionally or not. Does Swift consciously pepper her compositions with T Drops? It is difficult to say. With composers like Bach, the intention is clear. It's hard to argue that he did not know exactly what he was doing with his four-note signature. Ditto whenever the rapper Birdman does his trademark "brrrr" birdcall, as in "What Happened to that Boy," his 2003 hit featuring Clipse. The

T Drop on the other hand, may not be a deliberate inclusion in Swift's songs, but that does not mean it should be taken any less seriously.

The T Drop allows us to focus on Swift's songcraft in a way that popular appraisals of her work often ignore. "Blank Space" was a smash in 2014, praised by the *New York Times* as Swift's "funny and knowing" response to tabloid obsessions over her love life. No critics commented on *why* her song was so effective, though, preferring to use the opportunity to further discuss that same tabloid gossip. But a bit of musical analysis can give us the insight we need. The "knowingness" that critics detected in "Blank Space" lies in the way that each element of the song is meticulously constructed. After Swift sings the lyric in the chorus, "I've got a blank space, baby," she pauses (1:20). At the same moment, every instrument in the song drops out, leaving Swift's voice all alone in a literal "blank space" to sing the chorus's kicker, "and I'll write your name." In another detail, when Swift sings "I can make all the tables turn" at 1:52, the track's bass line suddenly goes *in the opposite direction* from what it had been doing in the song up to this point. Small moves like this convey big meanings. Swift becomes a knowing narrator by demonstrating her musical control over the song.

Ignoring Swift's musical craft is tantamount to ignoring her agency as an artist, and it undervalues the labor and invention of pop songsmiths. Swift's contemporary, the performer and composer Ellie Goulding, complained about the critical reaction to her 2015 song "On My Mind," when journalists speculated whether the song was about a famous ex: "It's like, you can be a great artist, you can write great songs, but the thing that everyone is going to talk about is some relationship they think you have had or not had." In discussing this with her friend Swift, both musicians concluded that "it's definitely something we both think happens to female artists over male artists." The scholar Kristin Lieb agrees with Goulding's assessment, stating in her study on gender and branding in the music industry that women "must harness the power of personal narrative to construct, maintain, and extend their career lifestyles." Whereas Maroon 5 lead singer Adam Levine, for instance, can change how and what he writes on each successive album and not worry about critics interpreting each new phase as evidence of his shifting personal life, female pop stars often are not given the same freedom. As such, artists like Swift, Goulding, Beyoncé, Gaga, and many others find ways to assert creative control over the narratives laid on their work. "I can read you like a magazine," Swift sings on "Blank Space," which is to say: not at all.

Swift makes one of her boldest creative choices in the hit "Love Story" from 2008. A retelling of Shakespeare's *Romeo and Juliet*, "Love Story" features a surprising deviation from the source material. As Swift explained, Romeo and Juliet "is one of the best love stories ever told, but it's a tragedy. I thought, why can't you . . . make it a happy ending and put a key change in the song and turn it into a marriage proposal." Swift did just that, modulating up two keys for the song's finale (see Chapter 10 for an explanation of modulation) and revealing that Juliet's father gave her the go-ahead to wed Romeo (it is left unclear how this development affected the ongoing Montague-Capulet feud). Swift was not the first composer to rewrite the ending of *Romeo and Juliet*. Russian composer Sergei Prokofiev did the same thing during 1930s when he composed a ballet based on Shakespeare's tragedy, giving a different reason than Swift for changing the ending of his version: "Living people can dance, the dying cannot." Stalin's government did not approve of the change, however, deciding that the composer required "ideological guidance," a phrase that appears even more chilling for the banality of its language. Prokofiev's producer asserted that it was not worth his own death "so that Romeo and Juliet should live," and reverted back to the original, tragic, double-death before the ballet's 1940 USSR premiere.

Swift did not have to stand up to an authoritarian dictator after penning "Love Story," but something tells us she would have. From the T Drop to her rewriting of Shakespeare, Taylor Swift is a composer determined to write songs of deep musical integrity. She uses the notes of ancient scales in ways that make their pitches sound brand new, ensuring that no matter what prefabricated identity the gendered expectations of the music industry will force her into next, her underlying songcraft will shine through in subtle statements of melodic truth.

3

The Harmonic Hero's Journey

Harmony: Fun ft. Janelle Monáe—"We Are Young"

"We Are Young" (2011) is one of the more peculiar songs to have occupied the top spot on the Billboard Pop Charts. When the chorus hits, there is no doubting the track's #1 bona fides: soaring vocals, grooving drums, and an anthemic promise to "set the world on fire." The feeling of youth is palpable, exhilarating—the chorus is something to play on endless repeat. But before they get to the chorus, listeners must first make our way through the verse, which exists in an altogether different universe: jittery vocals, martial drums, and dark lyrics detailing depravity, drugs, and scars.

There are two ways to interpret the song's rise to the top of the charts. Songsmiths Nate Ruess, Jack Antonoff, Andrew Dost, and producer Jeff Bhasker succeed either in spite of the bizarre, bifurcated structure of their work, or because of it. We lean toward the latter explanation. The feeling of youthful invincibility in the chorus of "We Are Young" is made that much sweeter precisely because it follows the decidedly grown-up and jaded

"We Are Young" performed by Fun featuring Janelle Monáe, written by Jack Antonoff, Nate Ruess, Andrew Dost, Jeff Bhasker, Fueled By Ramen, 2011.

narrative in the verses. Each time the song veers from verse to chorus, listeners are moved from adult woes to childlike wonder. The chorus is brash, bold, and clear. The verse is restless, uncertain, perhaps a bit inebriated. At the very start of the song, Ruess slurs his sentences, stuttering the word "I" in a way that might convey nervousness or drunkenness. Pounding tom-toms accompany his unstructured monologue, perhaps foreshadowing the pounding headache sure to come for our narrator. Stressed urgency pervades the verse as he stumbles over the word "I." It is not just the lyrics that give the verse this rushed feeling. The section is literally rushed, a full 24 BPM faster than the chorus to come. The first verse pulses at 116 BPM, the chorus at 92 BPM, and the second verse slows down to somewhere in between the two, at 96 BPM. Then the pulse returns to 92 BPM for the second chorus, where it remains for the rest of the track. This kind of midstream tempo-jumping is not unheard of in popular music, but it is uncommon. The effect is disorienting and undesirable for the purposes of, say, getting people moving on the dance floor. Like the metric shifts in "Hey Ya!" examined in Chapter 1, the tempo changes in "We Are Young" make for an unusual feature that give the song a unique identity, here one of careening between emotional states. Each time the music pauses before the chorus and the BPM drops down, the song settles into an optimistic mood. "Tonight"—or at least until the tempo changes again—"we are young."

Tempo shifts are just one of the ways that Fun differentiates between verse and chorus. The declamation—the way in which words are set to music—changes radically between each section. In Chapter 2, we noted how Taylor Swift makes use of melisma in "You Belong with Me," the technique of stretching a single syllable out over multiple pitches. There, Swift stretched the single syllable of "see" into a lengthy three: "see-ee-ee." In the chorus of "We Are Young," Ruess and Fun put Swift's three-syllable

FIGURE 3.1 "Tonight" stretched out with melisma.

melismas to shame (Figure 3.1). The first word, "tonight," is not really "tonight" at all. In Ruess's reading, it becomes "to-ni-ii-ii-ii-ight." On the repeat of the chorus, at 1:09, the melisma stretches further: "to-ni-ii-ii-ii-iiii-ii-ii-ii-ight."

It's rare to sight a decasyllabic melisma in the wild, but Ruess is not even close to finished. Further melismatic transformation can be spotted at the end of each chorus, with even more extreme vowel play, a simple "sun" becoming "sunnnn-oh-ah-oo-wuh-uh-un"—or something to that effect. The melismas here are entertaining, but they also serve an important musical function. In contrast to the chorus, the declamation in the verse is almost entirely syllabic, with each syllable of text set to a single note of music. Most pop songs use syllabic declamation. Melisma, though, can make familiar words or phrases sound suddenly new and rich with meaning. That is why melisma is so often used in sacred music. The chant "Viderunt Omnes" as set by the medieval French composer Pérotin is an excellent example: the first syllable, "Vi-," is stretched out over 109 separate pitches before moving on to the "de-" of "Vi-de-runt." But Pérotin has nothing on the chanting of Sufi mystics, who can stretch out the word "Allah" for hours on end. From religious chant to "We Are Young," extended melisma brings listeners and performers deeper into the meaning and texture of lyrics, saturating common words with fresh resonance.

There is another musical technique that deepens the chasm between verse and chorus in "We Are Young." In order to understand why the song's chorus is so undeniably thrilling, we must delve into the world of tonal harmony to hear how Fun draws new meaning from one of the oldest chord progressions in the modern pop canon. Melody describes multiple pitches being sounded out one at a time, and **harmony** describes multiple pitches sounding at the same time. Harmony takes many forms, and one of the most important in a pop context is its function as accompaniment to a melody. A common expression of harmony is a **chord**: a stack of notes—three or more—that are sounded together. Chords are like musical wallpaper. Hang a musical melody against a different harmonic scheme and though the melody won't change, our perception of it will. Like wallpaper, chords come in a number of variations: major, minor, diminished, augmented, suspended—each one producing a different kind of backdrop for a melody. Most twenty-first-century pop music relies on major and minor chords, and "We Are Young" is no exception. Major and minor provide a very specific type of background shading, and the two are understood as diametrically opposed. Major chords, on the whole, conjure more positive feelings, while minor chords tend to project more melancholy emotions. We will explore the science and culture of major and minor further in later chapters; suffice it to say for now that major chords tend to color a melody as bright and happy, minor chords as dark and sad.

An excellent example of harmony's colorful qualities can be found in another song by the artist we explored in the last chapter, Taylor Swift. The chorus of "Shake It Off" (2014) features the exact same melody line sung three times in a row, each time with different lyrics: "Players gonna play play play play play/ Haters gonna hate hate hate hate hate/I'm just gonna shake shake shake shake shake." The lyrics are not the only thing that changes with each repetition, though—so do the chords that harmonize the melody. The first time, Swift uses a minor chord. The second time, a major chord. The third time, a different major chord. Each chord gives the melody a different backdrop, so that the repeating phrase stands out against the changing harmonic wallpapers. Just like that, what could be an entirely boring, repetitive chorus turns endlessly engaging as each harmonic shift gives new color and meaning to the unchanging melody, arcing the chorus from darkness to light without altering a pitch in Swift's vocal line.

In the chorus of "We Are Young," chords become more than wallpaper, as Fun turns static harmony into moving melody. The band is able to do so thanks to a way of musical thinking first described in 1722 by Jean-Philippe Rameau, the French composer and theorist whose *Treatise on Harmony* flipped the musical script and earned him the title "The Isaac Newton of Music." Like Newton, Rameau took an abstract phenomenon in nature and named and codified it. Rameau proposed that harmonies could move like melodies if you recognized that within each chord there is a single, root pitch that defines the sound of the chord called the "fundamental bass." Once musicians began thinking of chords as having a fundamental pitch, then they could begin to structure harmonies horizontally, like melodies—one chord after another. One of Rameau's biographers describes him as "obsessed" by the horizontal dimension of harmony, its capacity for forward motion. Chords could begin to tell their own stories. Almost 300 years later, the chorus to "We Are Young" now features two musical dramas unfolding at once. One is the melody sung by Ruess, which lays out notes from the major scale one by one. The other is the **chord progression**, the sequence of harmonies played by Antonoff on bass and Dost on piano. Following in Rameau's footsteps, the members of Fun understand that just as certain melodic patterns stir our emotions, so do certain chord progressions.

We need one more concept in our musicological utility belt before we can dive back into "We Are Young," and it is the part of Rameau's treatise that he called **tonality**. Here is the idea: a scale is a collection drawn from the twelve pitches in an equally divided octave, but every pitch in the scale is not equally important. In tonality, the pitch that is most important is the first one in the scale, called the **tonic**. Metaphorically speaking, this first note of a scale represents its tonal home, the place to which the other pitches want to return. In turn, the chord built up from this tonic pitch is called the tonic chord and represents a song's home, the harmonic center of a given song. In tonality, the drama comes from leaving the home chord and then figuring out how to return. Classical composers understood the importance of this new tonal system and paid due respect to the tonic harmony when naming their compositions. Hence, Mozart's Symphony 41 in *C major*, Tchaikovsky's Symphony 6 in *B minor*, and so on.

"We Are Young" uses the F major scale, which means its tonic chord is F major. In the chorus, this is the first chord we hear, under the lyrics "Tonight, we are . . ." On the next word, "young," the progression moves to a D minor chord. Already we have traveled far away from our tonal home of F major (Figure 3.2). The feeling of homesickness is palpable. Nate Ruess is singing about being young, but suddenly we do not feel young at all. With a minor harmony ringing out, it feels like we're lost in the woods. In the next lyric, "so let's set the world on fire," the melody looks for an escape route, sailing up into the higher part of Ruess's vocal range on the word "fire." At this moment, something promising happens. The word "fire" features another harmonic shift, this time to a B-flat major chord. The change is encouraging, a burst of major harmony catalyzing hope and possibility. "We can burn brighter," the melody continues. Can we? It depends on the next harmony to come. The suspense is brutal. The lyrics continue, "We can burn brighter than the sun," and right on "sun" the final chord in the chorus progression appears, and it holds our fate in its hands. Will it be major or minor? The first, major, promises

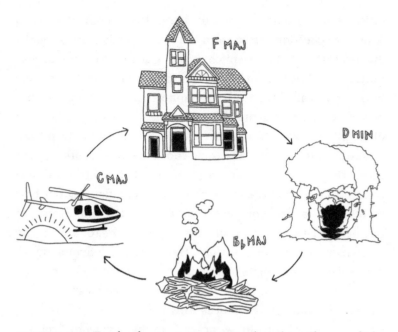

FIGURE 3.2 The chord progression journey: the safety of home, a dark turn in the woods, a signal for hope, and the joyous rescue.

confirmation of the chorus's early optimism. The second option, minor, signals despair, bringing to mind the myth of Icarus: have we been flying too close to the sun? Luckily, when Ruess lands on the lyric "sun," we hear a C major chord. Hallelujah. We've been rescued. C major is the chord that will airlift us back to our tonal home. The harmony shifts back to F major. A repetition of the chorus is under way, and the chord cycle begins anew: "Tonight, we are young . . ."

Each chorus of "We Are Young" represents an epic harmonic journey over the course of twenty-one seconds. The four chords in the progression—F major, D minor, B-flat major, C major—add color to the melody while narrating their own tale of tonal distance and return. Fun is far from the first band to realize the power of this particular progression, as these four chords have carried us through almost a century of pop music. Composed in 1934, Rodgers and Hart's "Blue Moon" was one of the first songs to use the progression. When Elvis repopularized the song in a 1956 recording, it generated so many imitators that the chord changes became known as the "'50s progression." Less flatteringly, it also earned the name "ice cream changes" thanks to the overly saccharine style of many hits that adopted it. This chord progression has been used an incalculable number of times since, spanning musical styles from pop to country to hip hop to rock, a musical link connecting such disparate material as Whitney Houston's "I Will Always Love You" (1992), Rebecca Black's "Friday" (2011), Ben E. King's "Stand By Me" (1961), Justin Bieber's "Baby" (2010), Bobby Pickett's "Monster Mash" (1962), and DJ Khaled's "I'm the One" (2017).

As "We Are Young" signals, the '50s progression shows no signs of stopping. Its four chords are as straightforward as they are unavoidable, and songwriters will continue to find new lyrics and melodies to draw on its narrative power. The "ice cream changes" are not unusual for their staying power, either. There are many standard chord progressions that have shown remarkable resilience over the years. The 12-bar blues progression is another bedrock of American popular harmony. Refined by African American musicians in the Mississippi Delta at the start of the twentieth century, it undergirded countless hits of the 1940s, '50s, and '60s. Today, the 12-bar blues is less pervasive than the '50s progression, though it shows up in surprising places, like Weezer's 2018 track "Can't Knock the Hustle." Another influential progression, known simply as "rhythm changes," emerged from George Gershwin's 1930 smash hit "I Got Rhythm" and became the foundation for countless jazz compositions. There is even a chord progression called the Axis that is made up of the same chords as "We Are Young," but laid out in a different order: D minor, B-flat major, F major, C major. What may appear to be a trivial rearrangement shifts the progression to a completely new musical world—one that will be explored in depth in Chapter 14.

Despite the proven power of chord progressions, some of the most successful pop songs eschew harmonic changes altogether and use only a single chord from start to finish. The infectious rhythm of "Bo Diddley" (1955), by the eponymous rocker, launched a thousand imitators, even though the song hung on to the same G major chord throughout. The Temptations' "Papa Was a Rolling Stone" (1972) lasts a staggering twelve-plus minutes in its original album version, without ever diverging from B-flat minor. How is this possible? The Temptations add voices and instruments one by one, slowly building up the narrative of an absentee dad to create a sense of exquisite loss. The lack of harmonic change creates a gulf between the five Temptations and the father figure. While he travels far and wide, they are stuck in place, both geographically and harmonically.

Whether a single chord or a hundred, the strength of a chord progression comes not from its originality but from the way it is used. "We Are Young" derives its power from the harmonic journey of its chorus, but it only works because every other musical element supports the song's overall arc from dark, paranoid verses to uplifting, nostalgic choruses. The verse plunges listeners into adulthood like an ice-water bath, while the chord progression of the chorus takes listeners back in time to a simpler era of "ice cream changes." On the heels of "We Are Young," Fun's Jack Antonoff charted a career as one of the most in-demand young producers in pop, working with everyone from Lorde to Taylor Swift to St. Vincent. The stark difference between verse and chorus in "We Are Young" is representative of one of Antonoff's songwriting maxims, which he in turn cribbed from Bruce Springsteen: "Blues in the verse and gospel in the chorus."

The musical and lyrical differentiation between verse and chorus in "We Are Young" gives the song a productive tension, but ultimately the song reached the top of the charts because it leans over into nostalgic innocence. In the end, the gospel outweighs the blues. Besides the chorus, there is an additional bridge section in the song that communicates youthful optimism starting at 2:32. At this moment, a choir suddenly appears, along with the unmistakable voice of Janelle Monáe. She repeats a single phrase while the choir sings a wordless melody, "La la/la la la la/La la/la la la la." The band overdubbed close to forty separate vocal takes to create the effect of a giant choir. This massive sound echoes a later lyric in the song: "I can hear the choir." Listen closely, and one other element of youthful nostalgia emerges from the chorus: the choir is a children's choir. Who needs angels when you have the beatific voices of twenty Los Angeles school kids?

"We Are Young" is so effective because it generates an overwhelming sensation of lost youth, regained anew each time the chorus hits. The entire arc of the song mirrors the timeless chord progression in the song's chorus, which begins on a major tonic, dips down to a worrisome minor chord, climbs back up to another major chord, and then another, before triumphantly returning to the tonic home. The final moments of the song suggest a kind of synthesis between the song's disparate verse and chorus, between past youth and present adulthood. The last lyrics of the song are nearly identical to those that occur in the verse just before the first chorus at :40, "I'll carry you home." When the lyric returns at the end of the song, though, there is an addition: "I'll carry you home *tonight*." With that added word, present and past merge, suggesting a reconciliation between the song's split personalities and musical divergences. Tonight, we can be young and old and all things at once, as long as the harmony keeps going.

4

When the Drop Broke the Pop Song

Form: Rihanna ft. Calvin Harris—"We Found Love"

Until the end of the chorus, the form of "We Found Love" (2011) behaves like the form of any other pop song. But after Rihanna sings the title lyric "We found love in a hopeless place" for the fourth and final time, something extraordinary happens. Like the upward slope of a rollercoaster, every moment of the next section is dedicated to building tension. At :52 a forceful snare drum enters, hammering out an insistent rhythm. From a distance, another snare starts up, increasing in volume and speed, like the clicking gears of the rollercoaster ratcheting faster and faster. In the background, white noise whooshes like a gust of wind. Sonic energy builds into a storm. Both snares meet at full volume, bouncing off each other. A screeching synthesizer rises up, bending toward the song's tonal home. Another rising synth joins. Tension accrues in every element. The suspense grows exponentially, the anticipation almost too much to bear—it has to stop! And then, at 1:07, it drops.

"We Found Love" performed by Rihanna featuring Calvin Harris, written by Calvin Harris, Def Jam, 2011.

A booming kick drum pounds out every beat, a technique dubbed "four to the floor." The low frequencies of the bass are loud enough to shake your bones. All the song's textures unite around an irrepressible groove. Rihanna, meanwhile, is nowhere to be found. This section is not about lyrics, it's about dance—at least until it ends at 1:22. Then, the energy decreases as Rihanna reenters to sing the next verse. But anyone listening is still buzzing from the rush created by Rihanna and Calvin Harris's use of the **build** and **drop**. The sections are two sides of the same coin: the build generates pent-up energy and the drop releases it, all but requiring listeners to bounce up and down in fifteen seconds of ecstatic joy.

The excitement in "We Found Love" doesn't just lie in the musical energy of the build and drop, but in the fact that their presence breaks expectations of pop **form**. Form describes the large-scale musical structure of a composition and the way it can be broken down into different **sections**. If we think of a song like a short story, then each section would be a paragraph, each melody a sentence, each pitch a word. Thinking about form helps us understand the dramatic arc of a song, its emotional peaks and valleys. And just as there are well-proven ways to structure a story, there are certain song forms that pop composers reuse again and again. The most common has a dull name, one that doesn't quite capture its importance: **verse-chorus form**. "We Found Love" actually follows verse-chorus form to the letter in its first three sections, until the build and drop appear. This is no accident. Rihanna and Harris lure listeners in with a predictable form, then pull the rug out from under them with a surprise eruption of sound. The bait-and-switch makes "We Found Love" the perfect song to examine both how the rollercoaster of pop form works, and how it might be changing.

The first fifty-two seconds of "We Found Love" are a textbook example of verse-chorus form. The song starts with an instrumental introduction, then at :07 Rihanna launches into the

verse. At this point, the song's overall energy level is still low, the only instrument a pulsating, synthesized organ. Rihanna's lyric sets the stage for a romantic encounter between two dancers in a dim nightclub who find themselves "standing side by side." At :22 the song moves into its next section, the **pre-chorus**. The energy increases as new instruments enter the scene. Another synthesizer doubles the original organ part, while digital hand claps connect on every beat. Rihanna's vocal energy increases too, her melody venturing into the upper parts of her range. Lyrically, she raises the stakes by exposing her inner emotional world, suggesting something magical is afoot on the dance floor. The next section, the **chorus**, is announced at :36 by two crashing cymbals and the dramatic payoff of the song's central lyric: "We found love in a hopeless place."

Each section of verse-chorus form carries out a distinct role. The verse sets the scene, the pre-chorus builds tension, and the chorus reaches a point of climax. Then, the whole process starts again: verse, pre-chorus, chorus. After that, there's often a new section called a **bridge**, which provides contrast. The bridge in "We Found Love" occurs at 2:07, when Rihanna repeats the lyrics from the first verse against a new, and ominous, musical accompaniment. The section provides a welcome break from the cycle of verse, pre-chorus, and chorus, and sets up a final chorus (or two) to bring the song to a close. Figure 4.1 shows the standard verse-chorus form as a rollercoaster, with all its attendant highs and lows.

Note that this "standard" form is far from consistent in actual pop practice. There are as many variations on verse-chorus form as there are songs. Sometimes the bridge is deleted entirely; other times a composer will leave out the pre-chorus. Verses often have different lyrics each time they recur, but not always; choruses almost always use the same lyrics each time, except when they don't.

FIGURE 4.1 Verse-chorus form moves like a rollercoaster.

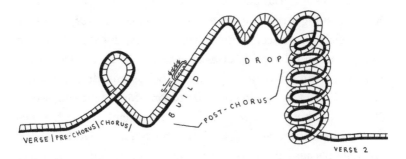

FIGURE 4.2 The build and drop interrupts and intensifies the verse-chorus rollercoaster.

Until the 2010s, though, most verse-chorus forms did share one thing in common: the chorus represented the energetic peak of the song. "We Found Love" disrupts that norm. The drop exceeds the energy of the chorus in thrilling, death-defying fashion (Figure 4.2).

The drop effectively usurps the role of the chorus, making that once-climactic section appear relatively tame in retrospect. The build and drop take the song's theme of finding love in a "hopeless place" and express it through an explosion of musical energy. But the build and drop don't hijack verse-chorus form completely. As soon as they're over, the song moves back to a verse as if nothing happened.

"We Found Love" wasn't the first pop song to inject a build and drop section, but its success made the technique increasingly common, leading us to ask: where did it come from? One clue to the section's origin lies in a key feature: it has no lyrics. This is an odd quality for modern pop music, which usually doesn't trust listeners to pay attention to music without words for more than a few seconds. The build and drop overcome such norms because the section is imported from the genre of electronic dance music, or EDM, where it was honed over decades into a failsafe recipe for musical euphoria. EDM is a catch-all term to refer to an array of dance sub-genres that have emerged since the 1980s: house music, electro, trance, techno, drum 'n bass, dubstep (to name a few). The sound and histories of each are distinct in their own way, but many of them make use of builds and drops, devices that arose as a way to add structure to long-form dance odysseys. EDM is all about encouraging body movement through slow-burning repetition, and verse-chorus form doesn't work well for the style because it compresses dramatic narrative into a neat, three-and-half-minute arc. There's too much change, happening too quickly, for dancers to get lost in the groove. EDM tracks unfold gradually over long periods of time, and builds and drops let DJs and producers introduce lows and highs into extended dance tracks without making rapid shifts. When Calvin Harris DJ'ed a set in Ibiza in 2015, one of his builds escalated for thirty seconds (twice as long as the one in "We Found Love"), and its drop lasted for a full minute (four times as long). Other examples can get even more extreme, as in "Strobe" by Deadmau5 (2009), an eleven-minute track featuring a six-minute-and-fifty-second build that reaches gut-wrenching levels of suspense.

The build and drop in "We Found Love" is not one that any raver would recognize. It's shortened to fit within a pop song. Thus, we propose a new term for this kind of drop: the **pop drop**. The pop drop became a common feature of pop in the wake of "We Found Love," showing up in Skrillex, Diplo, and Justin Bieber's "Where Are Ü Now?" (2015) and the Chainsmokers' "Closer"

(2016), among many others. DJ Snake and Lil Jon's "Turn Down for What" (2014) even *begins* with a build and drop! The pop drop has also exerted a more subtle influence on verse-chorus form, expanding it to allow room for other kinds of formal sections to insert themselves after the chorus. We can use the generic term **post-chorus** to refer to any section that follows a chorus. The music theorist Asaf Peres has done more than anyone to catalog the different kinds of post-choruses in modern pop, identifying the section across a diverse array of songs, including many covered in this book ("Chandelier," "Despacito," "God's Plan"). In each case, the post-chorus sustains or increases the energy level of the chorus. It super-charges verse-chorus form, prolonging its energetic high point.

Despite the increasing frequency of the post-chorus, Peres points out that most critics and scholars still view traditional verse-chorus as the dominant song form in the twenty-first century. Which is not entirely surprising, because while the sound of pop changes at breakneck speed from one generation to the next, pop form tends to move at a glacial pace. Since the start of the pop music business there have really been only three dominant formal structures. In the early 1900s, sentimental ballad form was common, using a series of repeated verses with the same music to spin extended yarns. "Danny Boy" (1913) offers a prime example, in which each successive verse reveals another layer to the tale of a son's long journey home. The repetitive form was still closely connected to folk music and proved ideal for storytelling, often in a flowery, nostalgic mode. In the 1920s, a new form with another prosaic name emerged: 32-bar song form. This was the age of industrialization in popular music, and the 32-bar song lent an efficient, assembly-line quality to songwriting. Dividing the form into even sections of eight measures allowed composers to churn out material from their perches on Tin Pan Alley, the now-fabled stretch of 28th Street in New York

City at the center of the music publishing industry. After a while, though, the form began to get stale. George and Ira Gershwin, the songwriting brothers who rose to stardom with 32-bar hits such as "I Got Rhythm" (1930), parodied its formulaic nature in "Blah Blah Blah" (1931), the lyrics of which run: "Blah blah blah moon/Blah blah blah above/Blah blah blah croon/Blah blah blah love." In the 1960s, verse-chorus form began to take over, a more flexible and individualized structure that a new generation of folk, psychedelic, and soul singers used to reflect their own idiosyncratic personalities.

Until "We Found Love," verse-chorus continued to dominate popular music, with no signs of giving way. But the pop drop and the post-chorus might change all that if they continue to expand and open the door to further revisions of verse-chorus form. If so, we may be on the verge of the first new song form of the second millennium, a narrative rollercoaster whose full shape hasn't yet revealed itself. What seems clear is that if the build, drop, and post-chorus are going to stick around, they will do so only by following the lead of "We Found Love." Rihanna and Calvin Harris's track is so effective because its EDM-inspired structure reinforces the song's message. The build captures the suspense of a first encounter, the drop celebrates the ecstasy of requited love. Together, they become a post-chorus that breaks the convention of verse-chorus form, mirroring how the song's protagonists break out of a hopeless place. While it may be hard to say if the pop drop is a permanent change or a passing fad, as long as the section is used to structure songs as uplifting as "We Found Love" we plan to enjoy the rush while it lasts.

A Voice without a Face

Timbre: Sia—"Chandelier"

Listening to "Chandelier" (2014) is like peering over the side of a skyscraper—a vertiginous experience. No matter where or when we listen, the effect is always overwhelming. What imbues "Chandelier" with this visceral power? One musical element drives the song: the sound of Sia's voice. Each time she sings, "I'm gonna swing from the chandelier," her vocal tone mimics the reckless, opulent acrobatics of the act. She starts on a shining high note, then swoops precariously low. She stutters as loose crystals fall to the ground, breaking on the marble floor below. She pendulums back up to the top of her range, and the chandelier glitters in the light. The song is alternately empowering and enervating, capturing the highs and lows of a woman deep in the throes of substance abuse. There is much to discuss about the use of melody, harmony, and form in "Chandelier," but to appreciate how Sia crafts the song we must approach the outer limits of analysis and investigate one of the least-understood phenomena in music: **timbre**.

"Chandelier" performed by Sia, written by Sia Furler, Jesse Shatkin, Monkey Puzzle, 2014.

Defining timbre is as difficult as pronouncing it (done like the French, "tam-brr"). "Tone color" is a phrase often used to describe the phenomenon, and we will use timbre and tone interchangeably. Timbre is the sonic quality that lets us distinguish between different voices and instruments. It is how we know our grandmother is on the phone when we pick up and not a telemarketer; and it is how we know Yo Yo Ma is playing a cello and not a kazoo. It is why Nate sleeps through the "Twinkle" alarm on his iPhone but always wakes up to "Old Car Horn," even when both are set to full volume. The emotional force of "Chandelier" is centered in the timbre of Sia's voice, which makes the song an ideal site to explore the phenomenon of tone. Like a swinging crystal chandelier refracting the light, Sia's voice runs through a vast spectrum of tonal color in her ode to the highs and lows of addiction.

How does timbre make all this possible? In theory, the scientific explanation for timbral difference is straightforward: every vibration creates a sound wave, and every wave looks and sounds slightly different (Figure 5.1). Simple waves, like those produced by striking a tuning fork, ring out bell-like and pure. More complex waves, like those created by blowing into a flute, produce

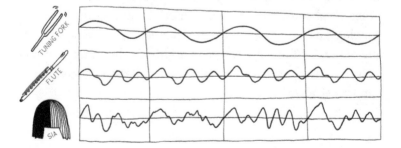

FIGURE 5.1 Soundwaves showing the same pitch produced by a tuning fork, flute, and Sia's voice.

overlapping vibrations and result in rich, resonant tones. Our perceptual understanding of timbre is so developed that not only can we tell one instrument from another but we can also identify different musicians who play the same instrument: one note is all it takes to know you are listening to John Coltrane and not Kenny G, even when they're both playing the exact same pitch on the soprano saxophone. In the same way, with just one syllable we can recognize Sia's unmistakable voice. Timbre is thus different from melody. It describes *how* one sings, not *what* one sings.

Despite our natural ability to perceive timbre and our understanding of how it's produced, we have limited vocabulary for actually describing the experience of listening to different sound waves. Timbre appears scientifically straightforward, but its mystery lies between the vibrations, in our emotional reactions to them. When we listen to Sia's voice, we are not thinking, "Gosh, I love how my cochlea tingles in response to the spectral overtone field produced by her intense larynx vibrations generated in the Rolandic operculum!" Rather, we simply say: "beautiful," "phenomenal," "unique," or "infinite"—adjectives all drawn from comments on the YouTube video "Sia's Best Live Vocals." This absence of descriptive language does not apply to other musical categories. We can determine with clarity that a melody follows a specific pitch pattern, that a harmony traces a certain chord progression, and that a rhythm matches a set of exact durations; but timbre remains an elusive quality of sound and music. Scholars have only recently focused efforts on systematically theorizing timbre so that we have more than vague adjectives to describe the sound of Sia's voice.

Throughout history, timbre has been a controversial aspect of musical practice. Anxieties surrounding gender and sexuality caused vocal timbre to be viewed with both reverence and suspicion. Throughout the eighteenth and nineteenth centuries, there was a sense that behind the alluring voices of operatic divas and *castrati* lurked moral corruption or decay. The women, of course, must be of questionable moral character in order to sing so sensually. The men had been physically altered as boys, castrated prior to the hormonal changes of puberty, and left in a bizarre, otherworldly state for the sake of the listening pleasure of others. One can hear an example of this prized, if perversely acquired, vocal tone on a haunting recording from 1904 of Alessandro Moreschi, "the last *castrato*." Over a century later, we still fetishize and fear timbre in equal measures, and timbre is the most hotly debated element in modern music, after lyrics. Sia is the ideal pop star to anchor an analysis of timbre in contemporary pop, because her stardom is based on tone alone: she is a voice without a face.

Sia's relationship to pop stardom can be described as ambivalent at best, toxic at worst. She has had as much success writing songs for others as for herself, and her ascent to the limelight was accidental, even unwanted. In 2011, Sia decided she would try "to be a pop songwriter, not an artist." Then two massive hit songs that she wrote and recorded as demos for other artists, David Guetta's "Titanium" and Flo Rida's "Wild Ones," were released under her own name, against her wishes. As fame became unavoidable, Sia chose to hide herself in various ways: by covering her face with her trademark oversize wig, by singing with her back to the audience, and by camouflaging herself on stage amid a sea of look-alikes. Counterintuitively perhaps, such tactics made her even more iconic. Amid the hypervisibility of her peers, "her ambition to remain anonymous ends up being what makes her recognizable." In turn, audiences focus in on her voice even more intensely, and her tone becomes her trademark. Pop scholar Robin James puts it succinctly: "Without gestural data from her, we have to focus on her musical technique." And her technique is something to behold.

To us, Sia's voice is like a stream, something you can step into, wade in, and even bathe in, but can't ever capture. During the quiet parts of "Chandelier," it behaves more like a gently babbling brook. When the song crests to its dizzying peaks, the stream starts to feel like white water rapids. Such metaphors are not as fanciful as they might seem. Sound travels as an invisible wave, but we sense timbre as a physical object. It has height, length, depth. Not only that, we actually "feel" timbre. Cognitive studies show that "motor resonance is involved in the processing of timbre, specifically 'noisy' timbral qualities." In other words, we have a physical response to timbre. Listening to rough timbres— think Lil Wayne, Tom Waits, or Macy Gray—creates a similar sensation in our brains that we get from touching something rough—think jute carpet, sandpaper, or an alligator's back.

The physicality of timbre is inextricable from our experience of listening to modern pop. Recording technology and digital synthesis have created ever more expanded timbral possibilities, as will be explored in depth in Chapter 13. Today, whole genres are based on the principle of vibrating not only the eardrums but the whole body. A Tribe Called Quest's maxim from "Jazz (We Got)" (1991) still holds true: "Make sure you have a system with some fat house speakers." During the late twentieth century, music took advantage of subwoofer technology to convey sounds at lower frequencies—from 20 to 60 Hz, the very edge of the human hearing—and at unprecedented volumes. Musical styles like Miami Bass privileged feeling over hearing, and are largely responsible for modern dance music's emphasis on deep, buzzy textures. The ethnomusicologist David Font-Navarrete explains that "although this spectrum of sound can contain fascinating melodic material, it is usually more tactile than auditory. It is felt more than heard." Miami Bass reminds us that pop music is multisensory. It can be olfactory, as in "funk," and it can activate the taste buds, like "sweet" jazz or "bubblegum" pop. The best proof of this maxim is found in the ways that deaf people listen: through touch, sight, meditation, and movement. The musicologist Jessica Holmes argues that the musicality of deafness illuminates the myriad ways we all experience music, since "sensing sound is not limited to vibration: vibration is rather a conceptual vehicle for understanding music as the transfer of energy across time, space, and bodies."

Sia understands the multisensory experience of music better than most pop stars and is a master of timbre, even if she operates by intuition rather than a carefully manipulated vocal technique. On *Carpool Karaoke*, the host James Corden asks her how she generates her signature sound, and Sia has no real answer. "It feels like I'm making it tighter or something?" she explains, gesturing to her throat. Perhaps this lack of technical understanding is essential to her craft, because on "Chandelier" she both embraces and defies established norms of singing, whether consciously or not. For one, she does not sing a three-syllable "chandelier" but a four-syllable "chan-duh-lay-eer," creating her own pronunciation. And each time she sings the line "I'm going to swing from the chandelier," her voice travels through a range of different timbres. The first six words are sung in a belting chest voice, a quintessential pop tone that Robin James describes as "overblown," as in, stretching the output of the voice to its limits. When Sia arrives at the titular lyric, "chandelier," she executes an astonishing run, sailing up to the top of her range over the course of the word and altering her timbre along the way, reaching the heights of the final syllable, "leer," in the celestial frequency of her "head voice": pure, limpid, and clear. She sings this melody once more, with new lyrics, repeating the same timbral journey. Next comes a melodic variation, and on the line "feel my tears as they dry," something extraordinary happens. Sia's voice seems to literally "break" at 1:04 on the word "dry," abruptly fading from raw vocal power to a ghostly breath and then instantly back. The same "breaking" technique can be heard in the voice of another powerhouse singer, when Adele sings the first verse of "Rolling in the Deep" (2011): "Go 'head and sell me out and I'll lay your ship bare/See how I leave with every piece of you." On the words "go 'head" (:19) and "how" (:23), Adele uses a "glottal flip," a technique that for the pop vocal coach Donna Soto-Morettini projects a "combination of vulnerability and defiance." The fact that Sia uses a glottal flip on the line "feel my tears as they dry" demonstrates the artist's intuition, because this may be the one moment in the song when we most "feel" the timbre of her voice as a physical sensation.

With impeccable precision, Sia generates a kaleidoscopic array of vocal timbres that display conflicting emotions: power, weakness, confidence, fear. An incredible performance of control and vulnerability, her timbral play effectively reinforces the themes of "Chandelier," a song that stands as a towering monument to falling apart. When she is not flying through the song's chorus, she is dealing with the stark reality of addiction, "holding on for dear life" in the post-chorus and withering under the harsh light of day in the second verse, chanting expressions of shame.

On "Chandelier," Sia's tone is half opera singer and half pop goddess. She breaks expectations of how women should sing, building up and then breaking down vocal convention. She would make the great opera composer Rossini proud each time she travels through the full range of her voice, ending on the clarion "-lier" of "chandelier." When she executes the glottal flip on "dry," however, Rossini would likely cough up his *affogato*. Women's singing has always been carefully policed. The German writer Georg Falck insisted in 1688 that singing must "flow from the throat and must not be thrust out in the manner of a female goat." In fact, musicians in the seventeenth century were so concerned with sounding like a "female goat" that they coined terms for the blunder in both French (*chevrotement*) and German (*Bokstriller*).

Comparison of harsh glottal utterances to the "manner of a female goat" points to deep biases surrounding how women's voices should sound (we have conducted extensive research on YouTube videos of goats and concluded that male and female goats do not bleat differently). Centuries later, these biases are still with us. The music critic Aimee Cliff observes that there is often a double standard at play when it comes to discussing vocal timbre. Male singers are free to indulge in *chevrotement*, screaming, crying, and bleating to their hearts' content, while women are criticized for the same. She compares the reception of Dave Grohl and Alanis Morissette during the 1990s, when Grohl was lauded for his "tireless screaming" whereas Morissette was pilloried for her "wild oversinging." Both Cliff and the writer Sasha Geffen celebrate Sia for creating a "growing space for women to be ugly, rough, and weird within what we consider to be pop," *chevrotement* be damned.

Though Sia helps liberate the tonal possibilities of women's voices on "Chandelier," the Caribbean accent she adopts in the song's verse and pre-chorus represents a complicated appropriation. On one hand, her use of an accent associated with black identity and colonial history could be viewed as an expression of intersectionality, the way scholar Osvaldo Oyola describes pop's "fake patois" as "a way for individuals to express their identity through solidarity, sharing a respect for that music's history as it is embedded in a framework of power." In other words, Sia's adoption of a Caribbean accent might mark a negation of her privileged status as a white, Australian-American woman and demonstrate her support of musical traditions marked by oppression. On the other hand, Sia's use of a Caribbean accent could be seen as turning blackness into a cultural commodity, effectively erasing the cultural and historical meaning of Caribbean music by reducing it down to a sellable sonic marker.

These are some of the ways that timbre plays a central and controversial role in modern pop, but it wasn't always so. Each era and place privileges different aspects of music. A quick run through Western art music history shows us that Baroque composers like Bach obsessed over melodic counterpoint, seeking to exhaust the possibilities of a musical idea. During the Classical era, Beethoven found his own obsession with melody, testing endless variations in sketch after sketch. In the Romantic period, Schubert and Chopin sought innovative harmonies through which they could build long tonal voyages. In twenty-first-century Western pop music, timbre reigns over all. Yet many non-Western musical practices have developed far more complex understandings of timbre over the centuries. For example, musicologist Kofi Agawu reports that in practices of Ghanaian drumming, the Southern Ewe have as many as seventeen names for different drum strokes, each one corresponding to a slight timbral variation. Western vocabulary for timbre is comparatively weak, but because it has become the most versatile tool of pop music we are starting to develop more expansive descriptions of timbral expression.

Pop invests in creating never-heard-before sounds in never-heard-before combinations. Timbre is the currency of modern pop, as Justin Bieber notoriously stated of his collaboration with Diplo and Skrillex, "Where Are Ü Now?" (2015): "It's expensive. The sounds we used are not cheap. They're very expensive sounds." Bieber was mocked across the internet for his comments, but we are here to say: the Biebs is right! There have always been expensive sounds, from Stradivarius violins to Steinway pianos, and it remains true today as producers spend endless thousands of dollars collecting newer, better, clearer digital sound packs and effects that can fine-tune the human voice. In Nicki Minaj's 2012 hit "Starships," for instance, the singer's vocal timbre in the song is sculpted like marble through a kit of pricey, space-age tools: Logic Pitch Corrector, Channel EQ and BitCrusher, Waves C1, SSL Channel, Renaissance Channel, De-Esser, Renaissance Compressor, API 2500, CLA Vocals, Doubler and VX1 Maserati Vocal Enhancer, Audio Ease Altiverb, Lexicon PCM Native Reverb.

Such digital massaging of the voice is now standard practice in pop. For vocalists like Sia, Adele, and Nicki Minaj, timbre is not only at the center of their art; it is the source of their economic success. Pop privileges timbre because it conforms with contemporary values of celebrity. Timbre is a musician's fingerprint, or more crassly, his or her corporate trademark, essential to selling records, concert tickets, and merchandise. With the barriers to recording technology rapidly collapsing and more music being released than ever, musicians' timbre is both their sonic identifier and their intellectual property.

Timbre is more valuable than ever before, and in our pluralistic society, the politics of timbral appropriation have become more sensitive than ever before. Pop artists can avail themselves of any timbre they please, but should they? Sia walks a fine line on "Chandelier." Her breaks, bleats, and belts blow up antiquated notions of a woman's "proper" sound, even as her Caribbean accent raises questions about the ethics of tonal appropriation. What is clear is that even in an age of limitless tone, our focus will always swing back to the voice. Sia's vocal performance on "Chandelier" reminds us that timbre is more than just sound waves—it is feeling itself. She creates a song that captures many of the central tensions of twenty-first-century life: substance abuse, gender politics, racial appropriation, and inescapable capitalism. Such is the power of pop at its peak—each timbral variation brings us deeper into the bittersweet musical universe of "Chandelier," where everything glitters brightly and yet is always on the verge of crashing down.

Painting a Musical Masterpiece

Lyric: Justin Timberlake—"What Goes Around . . . Comes Around"

Just when you think that Justin Timberlake has receded from the spotlight, he reemerges. From the Mickey Mouse Club, to fame as a Total Request Live (TRL) heartthrob with NSYNC, then a respected vocal producer, and now having matured into a pop icon, Timberlake regrooms his sound and image for each decade. Sustained by a steadfast hairline and immaculate falsetto, his sartorial choices have evolved over the years, from Canadian tuxedos, to suits and ties, to flannel. Few pop stars maintain such longevity, so what is Timberlake's secret? In each iteration, JT supports his changing image with an artistry for fusing the perfect combination of lyric and music.

If Timberlake were a painter, then "What Goes Around . . . Comes Around" (2006) would be his *pièce de résistance* because of its grandiose display of an essential technique that blends lyrics with melody: **text painting**. As Timberlake sings "what goes around, goes around, goes around, comes all the way back around," the melody follows the arc of his lyric. It's as if he

"What Goes Around . . . Comes Around," performed by Justin Timberlake, written by Timberlake, Tim Mosley, Nate Hills, Jive Records, 2006.

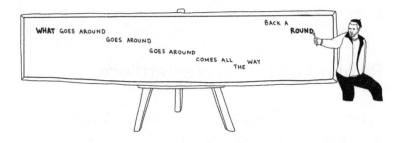

FIGURE 6.1 Timberlake text painting "What Goes Around . . . Comes Around."

starts his paintbrush in the center of the canvas on the home pitch of A, descends down as he repeats "goes around," makes a sudden upward brushstroke, then falls back to the starting note at the canvas's center on the final "comes back around" (Figure 6.1). The musical melody "paints" the textual meaning of Timberlake's chorus, making the song's sentiment more palpable and powerful for listeners. Text painting creates a literal connection between words and music.

Timberlake's love of text painting links him to the twelfth-century troubadour Bernart de Ventadorn, who used the technique in his song "Can vei la lauzeta mover" (When the lark beats its wings). When de Ventadorn set the line "beats its wings," he added a small "flutter" in the melody that musicalizes the airborne lark. Almost a thousand years apart, Timberlake draws from the same well, as have countless other composers and pop stars. Connecting Justin Timberlake to medieval troubadours may appear a stretch, but in fact JT has shown love for music of the Middle Ages in his discography. "Cry Me A River," Timberlake's first big hit from 2002, opens with twenty-five seconds of Gregorian Chant, a style of liturgical singing that dates back to the ninth century. The unexpected chant creates an appropriately somber introduction to Timberlake's lament for a broken relationship.

Text painting is everywhere, and it can be difficult to unhear once you know what it is. One example that now verges on cliché would be the practice of dropping all sound from a track when the lyrics land on the word "stop." Elvis Costello's "Alison" (1977), MC Hammer's "U Can't Touch This" (1990), and Nicki Minaj's "Feeling Myself" (2014)—among many others—are all guilty of using this on-the-nose gimmick. Skillful text painters can impart more subtle meanings, though, by creating an ironic rub between music and lyrics. In Lin-Manuel Miranda's "You'll Be Back" from the musical *Hamilton*, King George III tries to entrance the American colonists into sweet submission, singing "Oceans rise, empires fall/We have loved each other through it all." Blinded by confidence, he reveals his fallibility through inverted text painting. George's melody falls on "oceans rise" and rises on "empires fall." Both are backward, just like the Georgian monarchy. Unaware, he repeats this line over the course of three discrete solos during the show, revealing the fissures in the transatlantic relationship between the crown and the colonies. Through Miranda's text painting wizardry, the king's mistake becomes the audience's pleasure.

Like Miranda, Timberlake is something of a Renaissance man, his career spanning film, technology (he was an investor in MySpace), and fashion. Music is the foundation of Timberlake's success, though, and text painting lies at the heart of his sound. We can locate text painting at the start of his solo career in "Cry Me a River." As Timberlake sings "I bet you didn't think that [your plans] would come crashing down" the melody follows the words, descending the scale. Not that all his attempts have been winners. In "Can't Stop the Feeling" (2016) we find Timberlake leaning on well-worn tropes. There is a variation of the overdone "stop" text painting, in which the music stops at the lyric's command. At :42, the start of the song's pre-chorus, Timberlake sings "And under the lights, when everything goes." Right on cue, "everything goes," or at least the drums, bass, and background vocals do, leaving Timberlake's vocal, a soft synthesizer pad, and a lone handclap as the section's only textures. The move may be obvious, but it is no less effective, and and since the track was composed for the movie *Trolls*, we may give Timberlake some leeway. Elsewhere, the song displays more artful text painting. At :11 in the first verse, Timberlake sings "It goes *electric wavy* when I turn it on" over an *electric* piano modulating its volume with a wave-like tremolo effect (Figure 6.2). The moment marks a super-satisfying musical-lyrical blend, but the real payoff comes in the electric wavy dance moves that we get to improvise while singing along.

There are countless other examples across Timberlake's oeuvre, but "What Goes Around . . . Comes Around" takes the cake for its all-encompassing text painting. "What Goes Around," written by Timberlake, Timbaland, and Danja, is a masterpiece because it extends the first instance of its "comes back around" metaphor into a sort of karmic motif that pervades the entire song. In the vindictive lyric, the singer asserts that his ex's new romance is doomed because of an unspoken betrayal. Starting

FIGURE 6.2 Text painting a tremolo piano "Can't Stop the Feeling."

and ending on the same note, the circular chorus melody imitates the rise and fall of a relationship. As Timberlake sings "goes around . . . goes around . . . goes around . . . ," on each repeat he dips farther down the minor scale. Then, the melody jumps back up to the first note, as if to suggest that the ex-lover's new tryst will end abruptly for the same reason. The title fits the message. The melody fits the title. Together they establish a thematic pattern. Like oil paints meticulously layered one on another, the theme of love's revenge covers the song's entire canvas.

Peeling back another layer, we find other musical elements in the song that "go around" only to "come back around." Just as the chorus lyrics repeat the same phrase, the underlying chord progression loops throughout the entire song. The chords begin on a chilly A minor, followed by a series of deceptively cheery major chords (C major, G major, D major), only to round back to the A minor start. Often a songwriter will alternate progressions between sections of a song to create contrast, but here the chords keep looping back around, for the whole track—that is, with one important exception that we will examine later. Despite this regularity, the song never gets boring. Instead, we keep wanting more. Subtle variations in the arpeggiated guitar and orchestral strings provide just enough change to sustain our interest over this incessant loop.

Yet one more layer down, we find that even the song's overall form follows the "comes back around" theme. "What Goes Around" opens with a surprising instrumental texture: an *oud*, a Middle Eastern cousin of the lute—perhaps a nod to the text-painting troubadours of yore who accompanied their songs with lutes. At the start of "What Goes Around," the oud repeats a taut, percussive melody line four times in succession, with a stuttering variation the final time. From there, the riff continues. As the introduction builds, orchestral strings come in to double the oud, which plays through the entire introduction and then is cut off at :30, just before the vocal enters. We might be reaching to connect this abrupt ending back to the relationship at the center of the song, but it is not a stretch to say that this section finds itself stuck in a loop—it emerges, disappears, and comes back around. The "stuttering" repetition of the opening oud line reappears in the chorus. Between each of the repetitions of Timberlake singing "what goes around . . . comes all the way back around," the string section plays the stutter motif, as at 1:39. The oud itself, however, does not come back around again until 3:28 in the song. This time, the oud riff returns as a break, an energetic pause between choruses. As the oud loops, Timberlake ad-libs his "what goes around comes around" lyric. Every time we hear these words, we also hear the opening riff. Everything comes back around.

Over five minutes and twenty-two seconds, Timberlake paints his theme of relationship karma through lyrics, melodies, chords, sample loops, and song form—all to illustrate the pain of a breakup. Though the average pop song would have ended long ago, "What Goes Around" is far from over. Timberlake has not found closure. A question remains: what did his ex do to inspire this spiteful anthem? The answer comes after a final oud break at 5:15, which appears to point to the end of the song. But it's a fake-out. This outro is in fact the beginning of an entirely new section, beginning at 5:22: the karmic retribution. The oud riff continues, but instead of the string accompaniment, an unexpected synthesizer joins in, inciting musical unrest. This altered texture carries with it a new chord progression, a set of three ascending chords: C major, D major, then E minor. This looping progression rises, in contrast to the descending dominance of the "what goes around" melody. Deep bass and drum machines join in, building what sounds like a club dance track. Buoyed by the music, Timberlake lets go of what he's been holding close to his chest: "You cheated, girl." Now, it's her turn. In the final verse, his ex finds herself in a new relationship with an equally

FIGURE 6.3 Timbaland's text painting reversing "What Goes Around . . . Comes Around."

unfaithful partner. Now she's been cheated on too. Sealing the message, producer Timbaland chimes in with a final chorus of "what goes around comes back around."

This time, however, the "what goes around" melody is flipped upside down. Producer Timbaland sings "what" starting on a low note, ascends the scale singing "goes around comes back," then descends back to the first note as he sings "around" (Figure 6.3. By flipping the script of the original text painting, we can hear that our narrator has moved on. Karma has come full circle.

This final section of the song might represent the sonic aftermath of the relationship. It's a musical departure from what's come before, demonstrating the narrator's evolved emotional state while reprising and transforming the song's central lyric. This is not text painting as usual. "What Goes Around" updates an old practice to capture decidedly modern drama. More than a perfect pairing of lyric and music, the song blends the two together, keeping us hooked into an astonishingly long seven-minute pop opus—one big canvas coated in layers of text painting. And as if to sign his masterpiece, in the final verse, Timberlake seems to brag about his workmanship: "Let me paint this picture for you."

What Makes Pop So Catchy

The Hook: Ariana Grande ft. Zedd—"Break Free"

In 2018, legendary musician Quincy Jones embarked on a press tour notable for the candor he showed in discussing the many entertainment industry icons he'd crossed paths with over the years: Prince, Frank Sinatra, even Truman Capote. He joked that one of his daughters dubbed him "LL QJ"—short for "loose lips"—for his lack of self-censorship. One of his many barbs was aimed at Taylor Swift. Asked what he thought of the singer-songwriter, Jones responded, "We need more songs, man. [Expletive] songs, not hooks." This was a strange statement coming from the producer behind some of the most indelible hooks in pop music history, from the grooving triangle rhythm that propels the chorus of Lesley Gore's "It's My Party" (1963), to the call-and-response melodies between Sinatra and the Count Basie Orchestra on "The Best Is Yet to Come" (1964), to the cyborg-voice-bassline that powers Donna Summer's exuberant "Love is in Control" (1982).

Jones was no doubt being hyperbolic, but railing against Swift for her skill in writing **hooks** points to long-standing

"Break Free" performed by Ariana Grande featuring Zedd, written by Anton Zaslavski, Max Martin, Savan Kotecha, Republic Records, 2014.

squeamishness surrounding this little-understood musical element. Hooks—simple, catchy, direct—are critical scapegoats for wider criticisms against pop music. The hook represents a fundamentally different approach to composition than that used in jazz and classical music, where the objective is often to unravel a musical idea over the course of a piece by developing or obscuring the source material. Pop hooks have no time for unfurling. They have an urgent goal—to catch listeners. The metaphor implied is not necessarily a flattering one. Listeners, by extension, are fish. We are defenseless against the charms of a juicy, wriggling earworm.

Musicians agree that hooks are an essential part of pop, but there is no clear consensus on what a hook actually *is*. We can try to solve this mystery by analyzing a song that relies on one hook after another: Ariana Grande's 2014 hit "Break Free," produced and composed by Zedd (née Anton Zaslavski), Max Martin, and Savan Kotecha. "Break Free" is platonic pop. Brash, bold, unsubtle, every second is designed to hold your attention. Ariana Grande sings about breaking out of a stale romance, self-actualizing in the chorus: "This is the part when I say I don't want ya/I'm stronger than I've been before." The combination of Zedd's explosive, EDM-style production, Grande's virtuosic vocals, and Martin and Kotecha's compositional acumen would have likely resulted in a smash no matter what. But "Break Free" is special because it buries hooks in every crevice. Uncovering them offers insight not only into the song's success, but into the nature and function of hooks more broadly.

Musicologist Charlie Kronengold explains the hook in general terms as "a memorable feature or aspect, something that stands out in a song, something that distinguishes the song from others of its kind." We can add more depth to this description by establishing a taxonomy of hooks—the effort may not convince anyone that hooks are good and useful things, but at least we'll be able to hear with some clarity what they do. To our ears, hooks exist on three different levels, each distinguished by function. The smallest level is what we'll call the **motif hook**. A motif is a short musical phrase or idea, often repeated and rearranged throughout a song. A motif hook can be any brief, memorable patch of melody, harmony, or rhythm. Examples of the motif hook would include Lady Gaga's "Ra ra ah ah a-ah/Roma roma ma-ah" vocalizing in the introduction to "Bad Romance" (2009), the whistled melody that kicks off Maroon 5's "Moves Like Jagger" (2010), and the bass drum pattern that undergirds Beyoncé's "Single Ladies" (2008). Moving up to the next level of scale, we can identify **section hooks**. Section hooks are longer than motif hooks, covering whole formal sections. They usually occur during a song's chorus, as in "Happy" by Pharrell Williams or "Fight Song" by Rachel Platten (both 2014), but they can also take over other parts of the form such as the pre-chorus and the post-chorus. Katy Perry's "Roar" (2013) is an example of the latter, saving its section hook for *after* the chorus when Perry breaks the word "roar" up into a leonine cry, "rrrrrroh-oh-oh-oh oh-o-o." Finally, there is the **conceptual hook**, which refers not to a discrete piece of musical material but rather to a compositional approach in which the overriding lyrical theme is threaded throughout a song. Taylor Swift's "Blank Space" has a conceptual hook of sewing silence into different sections, and as we saw in the last chapter, Justin Timberlake's "What Goes Around" expresses the conceptual hook of "coming back around" in multiple dimensions of melodic text painting, harmony, and form.

Each type of hook—motif, section, and conceptual—is present in "Break Free," and each serves a different purpose in the song. Motif hooks are devices designed to keep listeners engaged, moments that demand "listen to me!" One example is Grande's line "I only want to die alive" that occurs right at the start of the pre-chorus (:21). There are a number of factors that make it stick. For one, the "I only want to die alive" motif starts much higher in pitch from the verse melody that preceded it. The higher pitch frequency cranks up the overall tension, raising the narrative stakes. The lyric is also effectively "framed" so that our focus is drawn to it. Right before she delivers the line, a choir of Ariana Grandes sound a single syllable, something along the lines of "hooh!" Eight seconds later, after finishing the couplet with "never by the hands of a broken heart," the "hooh!" returns, putting a button on the phrase (:29). By bookending the motif with two "hoohs!" the song seems to say "pay attention to this!" Then there is the ornamentation Grande adds to the first syllable of the word "only," transforming it into "o-o-only." This a particular type of melodic embellishment that's been popular in music dating back at least to the Baroque age in Europe. Then it was called a *mordent*, a term that comes from the Latin root *mordere*, "to bite." The "biting" sensation Grande gives us when she embellishes the "o" of "only" is one of the many small gestures in the song that hook listeners in.

Finally, the line grabs us because of its complete lack of sense. What does it mean to "die alive?" And since when do hearts have hands? These are vexing existential queries that nevertheless pale in comparison to the brain-twisting line that follows: "Now that I've become who I really are." That last word is not a typo. In the production stage, Grande originally disagreed with her collaborators about the lyric, protesting to Max Martin, "I am not going to sing a grammatically incorrect lyric, help me, God!" Martin insisted on sound over grammar, and Grande ultimately conceded, perhaps because Martin has written or co-written twenty-one #1 singles for stars including the Backstreet Boys, Britney Spears, NSYNC, Kelly Clarkson, Pink, Katy Perry, Taylor Swift, and the Weeknd.

Once again, Martin's instincts proved correct. Somehow, the rhyme of "broken heart" with "who I really are" actually works.

The rhyme pleases the ear while the grammatical faux pas adds confusion, perhaps even a bit of frustration, that the mind can't shake. Martin is known for penning lyrical blunders that succeed because they *sound* right in the song. In Britney Spears's ". . . Baby One More Time" (1998), he wrote the seemingly violent hook "hit me baby one more time." Martin thought "hit" was shorthand for "hit me back," as in "call me back." Painfully disconnected from contemporary teenage slang, this off-color lyric nonetheless led to a worldwide hit. Elsewhere, Martin has come up with such inscrutable lines as "I keep it ruthless when I get wet" (The Backstreet Boys, "We've Got It Going On," 1995) and "It's soring me up inside" (Leona Lewis, "Outta My Head," 2009), and yet he remains the most in-demand producer in pop. Author John Seabrook explains that Martin's awkward lyrics point to a larger truism about pop: "Though it's rare to have a pop hit without lyrics, the lyrics don't need to mean much." Most important is the sound, and Martin understands that sometimes "are" will be greater than "is."

Before we proceed, we need to issue a caveat. Like many musical phenomena, hooks are subjective. Some are undeniable, but others may vary from listener to listener. Take the descending, melismatic run that Grande unleashes on the last word of the line "on the highway to hell" in the second verse (1:24). It that a hook? It's certainly an effective bit of text painting (the melody line seems to literally descend down into hell) and a showcase for Grande's vocal control. But does it make the leap into "hookiness" for everyone listening? For us, the moment is arresting enough to qualify as "a memorable feature or aspect," but it may blow by without your noticing. Another aspect that could exclude the run on "hell" from counting as a hook is that it only appears once in the song. It's not a recurrent feature but a one-time thing. Some might argue that hooks need to appear more than once to be labeled as such. But sometimes those brief and unrepeated moments become the ones we crave most. Britney Spears starts

"Gimme More" (2007) with the infamous announcement, "It's Britney, bitch." She never returns to the sentiment, but she doesn't need to. We'll press play as many times as necessary to hear that defiant phrase again and again.

Disclaimers stated, we can level up from the motif hook to the section hook in "Break Free." As in many pop hits, the chorus is the central hook of the song: "This is the part when I say I don't want ya/I'm stronger than I've been before." The section rivets the listener from start to finish. First, it hooks through surprise. At the end of the pre-chorus, right on the squirm-inducing "are," white noise begins to fill the track, rising in pitch and intensity to suggest that the chorus will feature a symphony of instrumental texture. Instead, when the chorus hits at :36 we hear the opposite: a yawning absence. The only sounds present are Grande's voice and a solitary, muted synthesizer. Then, in syncopated rhythm, Grande declares, "This is the part when I say I don't want ya." Entering just a moment late, her delayed rhythm contradicts the lyric's conviction—"this is" and "the part when" both miss the downbeat of their measures. Meanwhile, the synthesizers play directly on the beat, creating a rhythmic dissonance between voice and accompaniment. It is not until Grande sings the word "say" that she lands on a downbeat and the vocal and synth accompaniment lock into step. The next line, "I'm stronger than I've been before" builds on this newfound confidence, the first syllable of "stronger" landing on another downbeat, and the line's melody taking Grande up and down in a soaring arc. Up until this point, every pitch in the chorus, save one, was pulled to a single note: B-flat. On "stronger," the melody suddenly explodes into motion. The rhythm and melody of the chorus thus move from hesitation in the first half to assurance in the second. This narrative micro-journey gives an emotional weight to the section. At the same time, it creates a musical structure that reinforces the song's message.

The chorus's move from hesitancy to confidence mirrors the central theme of leaving a dead-end relationship. This takes us to the level of the conceptual hook, in which the idea of "breaking free" is expressed musically throughout the song in gestures large and small. "Break Free" is more than a title, it's an *über-hook*. Pop titles have always been memorable, pithy, like a billboard advertising the song's payoff. Take the double entendre in Cole Porter's 1928 hit "Let's Do It." Porter's title is like Jazz Age clickbait. "Let's Do It" draws us in with sexual innuendo, balanced with a inter-species message of love: "In shallow shoals, English soles do it . . . Let's do it, let's fall in love." The song's escalating playfulness and single-minded commitment to showing that "everybody does it" makes it enduringly effective.

"Break Free" threads its own conceptual hook throughout the track. The first instance is right at one of the song's pressure points, the ungrammatical "are" at the end of the pre-chorus. The errant "are" and the white noise buildup coincide with an augmented chord that harmonizes this key moment. In Chapter 3, we stated that basic chords are made up of three pitches, together called a triad. The first note, dubbed the root, establishes the name of the chord. If the root is D, the chord is a D-chord. The second note determines whether that chord is major or minor. The third and final note binds the chord into what is called a perfect fifth—a round, open, and hollow sound that is consonant to the root note. But an **augmented chord** bucks this arrangement. It raises the perfect fifth interval by one step, piling two major thirds on top of each other and creating an extreme dissonance against the root note that generates tension and suspense.

Because of its harmonic discomfort, the augmented chord is rarely heard in contemporary pop music. We suspect Zedd is responsible for its presence in "Break Free" because he is one of the few modern producers to make use of it. An augmented chord appears in Zedd's song "Stay" with Alessia Cara (2017) at about the same place in the song as in "Break Free": right before the chorus (2:04). It may be rare today, but the augmented chord was more common in pop of the past. The Beatles used it as a favorite device to create suspense, featuring the chord in more than twenty songs. It's most plainly audible at the start of "Oh! Darling" (1969). The song opens on a suspenseful augmented chord, transporting the listener into the middle of a relationship crisis in which Paul McCartney pleads with his lover not to leave him—narrative suspense bolstered by harmonic tension. In "Break Free," Grande is on the other side of such a crisis. The augmented chord, sounding at the highest moment of tension in the song, dares her to break free from conventional harmony, and by extension, from her own lover.

A gambit at the end of the chorus marks another of the track's conceptual hooks. A buildup follows the lyric "'cause I can't resist it no more" (1:06). Grande's voice disintegrates into digital fragments as she echoes out the word "more." Rolling snare drums arrest the harmony, beating faster and faster: tik—tik—tik-tik-tktktktk. This kind of buildup is familiar—we heard it in Rihanna's "We Found Love" (Chapter 4), and it represents the universal cue for an EDM-style post-chorus drop. In Zedd's first hit "Clarity" (2012) there is a similar build at the end of the chorus (1:02) that leads to an extended drop replete with piercing synths and euphoric chants. Could the build in "Break Free" also lead to a moment of deliverance? Alas, no. In a surprising move, Zedd drops the drop and moves right back into the verse. It's a buildup to nowhere.

What is going on here? We expect Grande to "break free" into a post-chorus drop, but she is denied. The explanation only becomes clear at the end of the song, once Grande sings the final chorus. After reiterating the phrase "I can't resist it no more" at 3:15, the denied drop from earlier suddenly appears. Right as Grande sings the word "more" a new section begins, full of noisy synthesizers and pounding drums. The section represents the end of the song and the climax of the track, and this moment of liberation gives us the much-needed drop from the first chorus. The delayed gratification is a clever compositional choice. It means the song's narrative of breaking free doesn't come easily—Grande has to earn her freedom. And by that point, the song has won us over. It gives us hooks at the motif, sectional, and conceptual levels that all work in tandem to make sure we will never forget "Break Free."

Returning to Quincy Jones's admonition that "we need more songs . . . not hooks," the analysis of "Break Free" shows us that songs and hooks are actually fairly inseparable. Hooks have been around since the dawn of pop. And "Break Free" may teach us something not only about pop but about Classical music too. At the start of the chapter, we insisted that Classical music follows a different playbook than pop, one that abhors straightforward, repeated hooks. Perhaps the assessment was too hasty. Even the bewigged composers of yore weren't above utilizing hooks in their works. The authors of *Songwriting for Dummies* cite Beethoven's Fifth Symphony as an example of an effective hook: "Da-da-da-dahhhh." And why not? Those four notes are probably better recognized than the biggest pop smash. When we start thinking of that iconic motif as a hook, the distance between Ariana and Beethoven collapses. Hierarchies of taste, class, and culture that separate Viennese Classical music from twenty-first-century pop begin to dissolve. The two styles become humble equals, existing only by the grace of the almighty hook.

Sometimes the Truth Don't Rhyme

Rhyme: Drake—"God's Plan"

Musical theater composer Stephen Sondheim has decried the decline of the perfect rhyme in his field. Playing his favorite role of the musical grouch, he laments that "listeners today have even lazier ears than those of my generation: pop music has encouraged them to welcome vagueness and fuzziness, to exalt the poetic yearnings of random images." In hip hop, too, the use of perfect rhymes has dropped dramatically over the past three decades. For some old-school rappers like GZA of the Wu-Tang Clan, the shift is symptomatic of a larger issue in the genre: "When you look at mainstream hip hop, the lyricism is gone." As the lyricists behind such elegant perfect rhymes as "The hands on the clock turn, but don't sing a nocturne just yet" and "I got mad styles of my own and it's shown when my hands grip the chrome microphone," both Sondheim and GZA have earned license to criticize. And criticize, perhaps, they should—there is no shortage of rhymes in modern pop that are alternately inane ("What are you gonna do with all this junk, all this junk up in this trunk?"), lazy ("I feel so lucky, you want to hug me/What rhymes with hug

"God's Plan" performed by Drake, written by Aubrey Graham, Ronald LaTour, Daveon Jackson, Matthew Samuels, Noah Shebib, Young Money/Cash Money Records, 2018.

me?"), and impenetrable ("I wanna fwoop, fwoop fwoop, but I'm broken hearted/Cry cry cry but I like to party").

If GZA and Sondheim were looking for a single pop star to embody the questionable state of modern rhyme, Drake would be a good choice. Adept at gaming new digital music platforms to break Billboard and streaming records, Drake has seen huge commercial success while becoming a poster child for the ills of contemporary pop. One reviewer compared Drake's flow to "catchy nursery rhymes" (they meant it as a compliment). There's a simplicity to Drake's lyrics that some find enchanting and others offensive.

Part of this comes from his frequent use of the simplest rhyme of all: **identity rhyme**. This is a rhyme in which the syllables of each word sound exactly the same—which is, basically, rhyming a word with itself. The chorus of "God's Plan" (2018) kicks off with a titular identity rhyme: "God's plan/God's plan." Identity rhymes mark key sections of Drake's biggest hits. The chorus of "Started from the Bottom" (2012) repeats the same line with a small variation, "Started from the bottom, now we're here/Started from the bottom, now the whole team here." So does the chorus to "Hotline Bling" (2015): "You used to call me on my cellphone/Late night when you need my love/Call me on my cellphone/Late night when you need my love." All these identity rhymes might be taken as evidence of a dashed-off approach to songwriting. One can imagine Drake producing material as quickly as possible rather than poring over each rhyme—especially since streaming services reward quantity over quality. Rather than paying artists by album, streaming services pay royalties out per song, making an incentive for shorter songs and longer albums. In response, Drake's singles inch close to an average of less than three minutes, while his albums sprawl past an average of eighty minutes.

Drake's savvy understanding of the streaming economy makes him a target for critics, but there's something undeniably effective about Drake's identity rhyme refrains. They strike a nerve, perfect rhymes be damned, because they reinforce the song's emotional beats. "God's Plan" is all about giving in to a higher power, so starting the chorus with an identity rhyme is a bit like reciting a mantra. "God's Plan" is an ideal site for studying the craft behind Drake's rhyming. In 2019 the track won a Grammy award for "Best Rap Song," cementing its status as a modern classic. We can better understand the song's success by examining its multiple approaches to rhyme, beginning with the rhyme scheme in the first verse of "God's Plan": "I been movin' calm, don't start no *trouble* with me/Tryna keep it peaceful is a *struggle* for me." The next two lines continue with the pair "*cuddle*" and "*lovin'*." What's notable is that there's not a single rhyme in the quatrain. At least, not a single **perfect rhyme.** "Trouble," "struggle," "cuddle," and "lovin'" are what are called **near rhymes**. Perfect rhymes begin with different consonants but share identical stressed vowels, and every syllable after the stressed vowel is identical. If Drake had paired "I been movin' calm, don't start no trouble with me" with, say, "Hey Fred Flintstone, I got Barney Rubble with me," "I always shave close so there's no stubble with me," or "Into telescopes? Check out the Hubble with me," then he would have made a perfect rhyme. Instead he chose "trouble" and "struggle." The two are *close* in sound. Near rhymes (also known as slant rhymes or half rhymes) share what the poet W. H. Auden called an "auditory friendship." Both have the same "truh" and "struh" start, but the ending "bul" and "gul" sounds differ subtly.

"God's Plan" is like a map showing how Drake navigates between perfect rhyme, near rhyme, and identity rhyme, because the song makes use of all three varieties. The decision of which rhyme goes where might be somewhat arbitrary, but there's a method to the madness. Perfect rhymes pop up in the chorus: "won't" and "don't." Their accuracy gives the section a chilly confidence. Near rhymes like "trouble" and "struggle" saturate the verses, as if Drake is gathering steam. As a bonus, Drake uses two types of identity rhymes. First, he repeats mantra-like phrases in the chorus ("God's plan/God's plan") and the post-chorus ("Bad things/A lot of bad things"). Then, in the second verse he rhymes different words with the same syllables—"know me" and "no me"—keeping listeners on their toes.

How is Drake able to switch between different types so quickly and with such ease? The secret lies in his strict adherence to melodic repetition. In the first verse, every lyrical line follows the same melody—ditto in the first chorus, and also the post-chorus. Hearing these melodies over and over produces an almost hypnotic effect in the listener, a sign of Drake's "nursery rhyme" approach. Even when the rhyme scheme shifts from perfect to near to identity, the melody never wavers, locking the listener into place. Drake's lyrics get deeper under the skin, moving from the sharp "won't" and "don't" to the plainspoken "bad things/bad things."

Drake is one of many modern musicians playing with rhyme types to communicate emotion, but it's an approach that took a long time to develop. When the popular song market took off in the late 1800s, perfect rhymes were all but mandatory. "After the Ball," composed in 1892 by Charles K. Harris, contains only perfect rhymes, but Harris, like Max Martin, often sacrifices syntax to achieve the feat. Sometimes he's forced to contort a phrase in order to get the rhyme to land, like in the lines "I had a sweetheart, years, years, ago/Where she is now, pet, you soon will know." "You soon will know" is a weird turn of phrase, but Harris needs it that way to make sure he hits the rhyme with "go." Not that anyone cared about the akwardness—the song was the first pop hit ever.

By the 1920s, lyricists were striving for perfect rhymes without disrupting natural speech. Composer Walter Donaldson and lyricist Gus Kahn show off their increasingly dexterous attempts in "Love Me or Leave Me" (1928), an influential entry in the Great American Songbook. Agile lines such as "There'll be no one unless that someone is you/I intend to be independently blue"—captured the wit and urbanity of the Jazz Age, and songwriters followed suit for decades.

Technology eventually unseated the status quo of perfect rhyme. Radio and records brought regional musical styles into the pop marketplace, and with them came near rhymes. Soon, the individualistic, imagistic, and colloquial language of southern rock and soul eroded the dominance of perfect rhyme. Once Little Richard blazed into "Rip It Up" (1956) with the near rhyme, "Well it's Saturday night and I just got *paid*/Fool about my money, don't try to *save*," there was no turning back. The era of perfect rhyme was over, the era of near rhyme had arrived.

Fast forward to the 2010s, and a single stanza of modern pop music might contain perfect rhymes, near rhymes, and identity rhymes—something singer-songwriter Julia Michaels accomplishes in "Issues" (2017). Michaels wrote hits for Justin Bieber ("Sorry," 2016) and other pop stars before striking out as an artist in her own right, and she mastered the art of manipulating rhymes during her stint as a songwriter-for-hire. She starts with an arresting couplet in perfect rhyme: "I'm jealous/overzealous." Then, an identity rhyme: "When I'm down I get real down/When I'm high I don't come down." Next comes a near rhyme: "I could love you just like that/And I could leave you just as fast." In the course of eight measures, Michaels deploys every type of rhyme, accentuating the soul-scraping lyrics. "I'm jealous/overzealous" becomes a taut, threatening phrase through its snappy perfect rhyme. "When I'm down I get real down/When I'm high I don't come down" sounds startlingly real because the identity rhyme has nowhere to hide. The near rhyme of "that" and "fast" might suggest the singer's steely nerve starting to crack. Michaels, like Drake, writes her own rhyming rule book.

Modern pop is the Wild West of rhyme. Today, artistry is less about creating a perfect rhyme than massaging the sounds of words to produce maximum emotion, as in the awkward-yet-unforgettable rhyme of "broken heart" and "who I really are" in "Break Free." Taking the practice to its logical end, some songs forgo rhyme altogether. Adele does this to moving effect in the chorus of "Hello" (2015): "Hello from the out*side*/At least I can say that I've *tried*/To tell you I'm sorry for breaking your *heart*/ But it don't matter, it clearly doesn't tear you a*part*/anymore." It's all perfect rhymes (outside/tried, heart/apart) until Adele throws in that "anymore," which topples the quatrain's neat order. But that's exactly the point. The lack of a rhyme adds to the melancholy surrounding a lost love—her broken rhyme shows us her broken heart.

The unorthodox approach to rhyme in Adele, Michaels, and Drake's music might unsettle elder statesmen like GZA and Sondheim, but it's a core element of the sound of modern pop. As Chance the Rapper has pithily put it, "Sometimes the truth don't rhyme." Still, the first time we heard "God's Plan," we thought it was a dud. Then the track quickly smashed one record after another on its release—4.3 million plays on Spotify and 14 million on Apple Music in its first twenty-four hours; according to Billboard, it racked up 82.4 million total streams in its first week. We were clearly missing something, so we called up someone with an encyclopedic knowledge of Drake's music: Jeremy Lloyd, one half of Marian Hill (with Samantha Gongol).

Lloyd theorizes that Drake's success with rhyme relates to his embrace of hip hop's turn toward singing in the mid-2000s, beginning with André Benjamin's "Hey Ya!" in 2004. Around the same time, the pitch-correcting hardware Auto-Tune, as made famous by T-Pain, presented rappers with digitized perfect pitch. This new texture enabled rappers who would otherwise never sing to experiment with melody. Singing rappers—once an oxymoron—made the blurring of hip hop and pop possible, and this has become a defining aspect of modern pop. Drake takes advantage of Auto-Tune to merge melody, rhythm, and rhyme together into a sort of "super hook" of hip hop flow and pop-song melody. The identity rhyme that starts the chorus—"God's plan/God's plan"—could have easily been rapped rather than sung. But Auto-Tune gives each "God's plan" a crystal-clear melody, reinforced by a verbatim repetition.

Drake's combination of melody, rhythm, and rhyme taps directly into human mechanisms of memorization, a kind of brain hack found across cultures. Neurologist Oliver Sacks explains:

> Every culture has songs and rhymes to help children learn the alphabet, numbers, and other lists. Even as adults, we are limited in our ability to memorize series or to hold them in mind unless we use mnemonic devices or patterns—and the most powerful of these devices are rhyme, meter and song.

Put more simply, when we hear repeating musical patterns, we remember them, especially if the repetition is embedded across melody, rhythm, and rhyme. Drake's "nursery rhyme" technique draws listeners in, but he's careful to keep it from being *too* simple. He smartly introduces an element of variation by placing the second "God's plan" on a different metric beat from the first (Figure 8.1). Displacing the motif from where we expect it to recur, Drake ensures that his repetition of melody, rhythm, and rhyme doesn't become too predictable.

By shifting the metric location of the motif, Drake keeps it sounding fresh without changing a note. It's an expert approach to identity rhyme, one that lodges the couplet in listeners' brains without ever boring them—with no fewer than fifty-four variations of the motif over the course of the song. Thanks to this, even though we didn't love "God's Plan" after one listen, we could

FIGURE 8.1 "God's Plan" identity rhyme, metrically displaced.

still sing its main hook. It worked on us despite our best efforts to forget it.

Drake shows that rhyme is an elemental part of the way we process music, and the "right" way to use rhyme was a controversial topic long before Sondheim or GZA's lyrical grumblings. In Britain during the early 1800s, Romantic poets debated the relative merits of perfect, near, and identity rhymes. One poet in particular shares much in common with Drake. John Keats liked to wear his emotions on his sleeve, and he could not make up his mind when it came to rhyme's virtues. On one hand, he celebrated it. By privileging sound over sense, he could let rhyme lead him to ideas that would not occur in prose: "Just like that bird am I in loss of time/Whene'er I venture on the stream of rhyme/With shatter'd boat, oar snapt, and canvas rent/I slowly sail, scarce knowing my intent." On the other hand, Keats recognized that a forced rhyme can dull the impact of an emotion: "The feel of not to feel it/When there is none to heal it/Nor numbed sense to steel it/Was never said in rhyme." Separated by two centuries, Keats and Drake might seem unlikely bedfellows, but the wordsmiths are connected by their ambivalent views on rhyme. When it spurs the imagination, "like that bird am I in loss of time." When it stifles an honest thought, "bad things/it's a lot of bad things."

Drunk on Rhythm

Syncopation: Kendrick Lamar—"Swimming Pools (Drank)"

If you happen to be reading this while wearing an analog wristwatch, or sitting in the vicinity of a wall clock, take a moment to glance at the second hand. You may notice something: the first tick seems to hang for a moment before the rest proceed at regular intervals. The effect is a product of our brain "slowing down" that first tick in order to process the information it is receiving. The brain does so through a process cognitive scientists call "subjective time dilation," which is another way of saying time is what we make it. That's why it flies when we are having fun, and drags on forever when we are stuck in line at the Division of Motor Vehicles. Music only exists in time. It can be flattened out onto a page through notation, but sounding music is an event, an experience. One of the greats joys of music is how it can make time elastic and erase the notion of objective "clock time."

As composer and psychoacoustic researcher Jonathan Berger writes, music *hijacks* our perception of time. Composers have taken advantage of this effect for centuries. Berger cites the

---

"Swimming Pools (Drank)" performed by Kendrick Lamar, written by Kendrick Duckworth, Tyler Williams, Top Dawg, 2012.

Romantic composer Gustav Mahler, whose song "Der Abschied" (The Farewell, 1909) seems to petrify time in amber. In modern popular music, hip hop is the genre that has best mastered the art of temporal manipulation, and Kendrick Lamar might be the most sophisticated time-jacker of all. Lamar has no small number of musical gifts. Like Sia, he is a genius at timbral variation, manifesting different characters and personae by subtly altering the tone of his voice, often multiple times in a single song. On tracks like "Swimming Pools (Drank)" (2012), produced by the Toronto-based beatmaker T-Minus, Lamar showcases another talent: his skill for creating temporal disorientation through rhythmic syncopation.

In Chapter 1 on "Hey Ya!," we explored the phenomenon of beat and pulse, and how composers establish metrical groupings of beats, then interrupt that order to create productive tension in their music. For our analysis of "Swimming Pools," we will zoom in from the level of metric grouping to focus on the spaces *between* pulses. Like most popular music, "Swimming Pools" uses a four-beat meter, and like all music, each of those pulses can be subdivided into smaller groups of two, three, four, etc. **Syncopation** refers to how much a musical rhythm stresses the subdivisions between each beat versus the beat itself. Low syncopation means that the rhythm of a song adheres closely to the underlying meter. An example of low syncopation would be the original version of the "Star Spangled Banner," which uses a three-beat meter and whose melody follows each of those beats almost exactly (see Chapter 1, Figure 1.4). Besides the initial "o-oh" and "by the," every syllable of "Oh say, can you see" lands right on a metric pulse. The result may not be particularly funky, but the temporal clarity of low syncopation is helpful for the kind of group singing necessary, say, in getting thousands of people in a stadium to deliver the national anthem at once (or, for that matter, in singing "Happy Birthday," another low-syncopation classic).

When it comes to pop music, by contrast, high levels of syncopation are the norm. Why we derive such pleasure from syncopation remains a mystery, but it likely has something to do with a phenomenon outlined by a study on music cognition: "Music's ability to send shivers down the spine is suggested to result from the violation of structural expectations." Pulse and meter set up strong expectations of rhythmic regularity. Syncopated rhythms that dance between pulses violate listeners' metric expectations, spurring a feeling of uncanny pleasure. Researchers have determined that our bodily response to syncopation operates in a U-shape relationship. Too little syncopation, and we do not experience a strong bodily response. This might be why it is so difficult to shake one's ass to the "Star Spangled Banner" (Marvin Gaye's version excepted). Too much syncopation, and the underlying pulse becomes obscured. The body cannot lock in. Between these two poles exists an elusive sweet spot wherein lies the groove.

Kendrick Lamar is adept at locating this sweet spot, and "Swimming Pools" offers a clinic in using syncopation to deny an audience's expectations. "Swimming Pools" is a cautionary tale of the dangers of excessive drinking and generational alcoholism, so Lamar's rhythmic play takes on additional meaning. Section by section, the song plunges listeners further into the temporal deep end as it accumulates more and more syncopated musical elements. This sonic plunge reaches its extreme in the chorus, as Lamar conjures the temptation of a dive into a swimming pool of liquor. Lamar's pool metaphor updates a lyrical trope used by blues and country singers since the start of the twentieth century: "If the river was whiskey and I was a duck/ I'd dive to the bottom and I'd never come up." Creating a twenty-first-century version of this escapist fantasy through a bevy of contemporary rhythmic techniques that defy our expectations, Lamar harnesses the inherent sensual delight of syncopation as a metaphor for the dangers of drinking. The feeling of temporal dissociation creates a high, and a warning. Lamar shows how easy it is to engulf oneself in pleasure, but once there, can you swim back to the surface?

"Swimming Pools" is designed to disorient from the start. The song begins on a slow temporal plane, with a haunting refrain that will return throughout the song. The instrumental texture here is sparse: a muted synthesizer roiling in the lower register, a solitary snare drum hit on every third beat, and two distorted voices that intone a ritual of inebriation: "Pour up (drank)/Head shot (drank)/Sit down (drank)/Stand up (drank)" (see Figure 9.1a). The first voice, reciting the commands to "sit down" and "stand up," is pitched down and sounds temporally "stretched-out,"

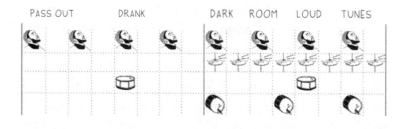

FIGURE 9.1 Kick drum syncopation, snare drum hits, hi-hat stutters, and lyrical triplets in the intro (9.1a), verse 1 (9.1b), chorus (9.1c), and verse 2 (9.1d) of "Swimming Pools."

whereas the voice repeating the mantra "drank" has been pitched up from its original frequency to sound unnaturally high and compressed. Do these voices represent Lamar's inner demons? The pressure of his peers? Whatever their meaning, the opening refrain places the listener in a mode of uncertainty. Making it clear that "clock time" will not apply in "Swimming Pools," Lamar and T-Minus disorient listeners through a sensory environment akin to inebriation by using various forms of temporal dissonance and rhythmic syncopation.

Like the currents that ebb underneath the ripples on the surface of a swimming pool, music can exist on multiple temporal planes. The kick drum that begins at :25 in the verse is the first strong element of syncopation. It strikes on the downbeat of the measure, then between the second and third pulses. This groove continues through the verse as Lamar's "natural" voice narrates a saga of multi-generational alcoholism. Halfway through the first verse, at :38, right on the word "dark" in the phrase "I was in a dark room, loud tunes," another rhythmic element appears: a hi-hat cymbal pattern ticking away at a rate twice as fast as the underlying meter (see Figure 9.1b). The hi-hat rhythm adds an additional temporal level to "Swimming Pools" by dividing each pulse of the song's meter in half. At the same instant, Lamar slows down his delivery, lowering the level of syncopation in his lyrical flow and landing the phrase "dark room, loud tunes" on each of the four pulses of that measure. Lamar here exploits one of music's unique properties. We are exposed to two different expressions of time simultaneously: the slow pulse of the song's meter in Lamar's vocal and the quick, ticking hi-hats. The interaction between each of the temporal planes creates a friction that grabs listeners like an undertow, pulling us step-by-step deeper into the waters.

Then at :51 the chorus hits and we are plunged once again into the deep end of a pool overflowing with syncopation. Multiple rhythmic elements explode into play: synthesized strings double the low, muted synthesizer from the opening refrain while cymbals crash on every first and third pulse. These added sounds increase the song's overall energy, as if cheering on Lamar's dive into a pool of liquor, and the chorus features one more rhythmic shift that completes the effect of total submersion. The hi-hats become unmoored from the rhythmic regularity established in the second half of the verse. They tick away at a steady double-time pace, and then, seemingly at random, they skitter off into impossibly fast trills and rattles, dicing the song's pulse into smaller and smaller subdivisions: three, four, even eight ticks to a pulse (see Figure 9.1c). In short, the hi-hat seems to go off the rails in the chorus, creating wild bursts of syncopation that raise the temporal dissonance of the song to a fever pitch.

After the intense high of the chorus, "Swimming Pools" cools off, returning to the song's introduction and stripping the texture down to a muted synth, sporadic snare drum, and distorted voices intoning "pour up (drank)." Things build back up slightly in the second verse, as the syncopated kick drum is again added to the texture and Lamar begins rapping—but Lamar's voice is no longer in his "natural" timbre. At 1:30, his voice is pitched up, compressed, and nasal, similar to the "drank" lines of the refrain. What's more, he is rhyming in the third person: "Now open your mind up and listen me, Kendrick." The song's engineer, Derek "MixedByAli" Ali, disorients the listener further by bouncing Lamar's distorted voice back and forth between the left and right speaker channels (listen on headphones and you will hear this clearly). Who is speaking here? The next line gives the answer: Lamar's conscience. The rapper's processed vocals suddenly take on new meaning. They represent a moment of clarity through an out-of-body experience.

But as quickly as the angel on his shoulder appears, it vanishes. At 1:43, halfway through the second verse, the "real" Kendrick reenters, his voice no longer distorted, panned, or third-person. He raps in a triplet pattern sometimes referred to as the "Migos flow," after the Atlanta trio who transformed the style into a trademark. In their song "Versace" (2013), Migos rap the three syllables of the titular lyric by dividing each of the pulses in the underlying meter into groups of three. Lamar does the same thing in the second verse of "Swimming Pools," splitting syllables into sets of three so that the lines "I see the feeling, the freedom is granted/As soon as the damage of vodka arrived" are heard as "I see the/feeling the/ freedom is/granted as/soon as the/damage of/vodka a-/-rrived . . ." Lamar's division of the meter into thirds would provide engaging syncopation on its own, but set against the hi-hat pattern of the second verse, the rhythmic tension becomes even more extreme. Lamar's triplet-based "Migos flow" creates another temporal layer by setting his *odd* division of the pulse into thirds against the hi-hat's *even* divisions of the pulse into halves (see Figure 9.1d). Lamar exploits the funky mathematics of intense syncopation, producing a division into groups of two and three *at the same time*.

Techniques like the Migos flow belong to the subgenre of trap music, which draws its name from a slang term for the illegal drug game and often features the kind of woozy, sludgy production we hear in "Swimming Pool." This is especially true of the hi-hats in the chorus, which rap scholar Justin Burton calls "the most iconic rhythmic element of trap in the 2010s," banging out "inhumanly fast" subdivisions that "sound like rattles." Since the 1990s, when the Houston-based producer DJ Screw began "chopping and screwing" his beats to stretch out or compress any sense of regular time, hip hop has leaned increasingly into hijacking time as a central aesthetic. The rattling hi-hats of trap have become one of its most frequent and powerful expressions.

Music critic Shawn Setaro has attempted to locate the origin point of trap hi-hats, and he cites the 1999 Juvenile track "Back that Azz Up," produced by the New Orleans DJ Mannie

Fresh, as the first appearance of the sound. Trap hats were further developed by producer Shawty Redd on the 2000 album *Causin' Drama*. In 2003, the term "trap" was coined by way of DJ Toomp's rattling hi-hats on T. I.'s album *Trap Muzik*. Producer Lex Luger refined the style further on the 2009 Wacka Flacka Flame album *Salute Me or Shoot Me 2*. By the late 2010s, trap hats had become a ubiquitous musical device, inescapable not only on hip hop tracks but even seeping into the musical vocabulary of decidedly mainstream acts like Taylor Swift ("Call It What You Want," 2017).

The popularity of trap hats has generated its share of backlash, not least for trap's associations with drug use and misogyny, but also for long-standing biases against the musical qualities of the genre. When we interviewed Dave Longstreth, lead songwriter for the rock outfit the Dirty Projectors, he remarked on his surprise when other musicians derided the sound of trap. For Longstreth, the expressive potential of trap hats proved revelatory: "The way that trap gives emotional and formal meaning to these new subdivisions . . . that's forever. That's a new vocabulary. Maybe the production will change, but those are amazing tools that are here to stay." Indeed, trap hats seem poised to become one of the defining pop textures of the twenty-first century, and as Longstreth suggests, it's an exciting exercise to imagine how they might further develop as a device. Already, artists such as Lizzo have combined trap hats with 1960s soul on tracks like "Cuz I Love You" (2019), showing that the hyper-modern sound can meld with classic pop in new and surprising ways.

Two distinct developments brought trap hats into the frame of contemporary pop music. One was the creation of the Digital Audio Workstation (DAW) software called Fruity Loops in 1998. Six years before Apple introduced GarageBand, Fruity Loops made digital music tools available to anyone with an internet connection and soon became the de facto platform for hip hop production. The success of Fruity Loops was somewhat accidental. Developed by the Belgian software maker ImageLine, it was a side product to their core hustle of producing pornographic video games like *Porntris*—which as its name implies was an explicit version of Tetris. But the popularity of Fruity Loops (since rebranded to the more "mature" name FL Studio) meant it quickly became the company's sole business. Fruity Loops was downloaded as a demo, pirated, and in some cases actually purchased by a generation of rising hip hop producers, including trap pioneers like Lex Luger and contemporary hitmakers like T-Minus. The rattling hi-hats in the chorus of "Swimming Pools" could be made in any number of the most popular DAW softwares—ProTools, Ableton, Reason, Logic, among them— but are a characteristic product of the Fruity Loops interface. Fruity Loops features an intuitive, easy-to-use step sequencer for programming drum beats that lays out a track's meter and all its possible subdivisions in a clear grid. By highlighting various subdivisions in the sequencer, producers can create Burton's "inhumanly fast" hi-hats with a few clicks of the mouse. Trap music is thus the product of a rich contradiction, using controlled, digital precision to create the pleasurable dissociation of wild, unruly syncopation.

The other millennial development that made the trap hats in "Swimming Pools" possible is more complicated, and something Lamar addresses head-on in his song. The temporal dissociation essential to the trap sound can be heard as a musical corollary to the rise of drug and alcohol abuse as a central theme in hip hop and a core part of the lifestyle for many artists. The woozy sound of trap is often linked to a specific drug, the concoction known as "lean," "purple drank," or "sizzurp"—a combination of codeine-infused cough syrup and soda—beginning with DJ Screw's chopped-and-screwed experiments of the 1990s. Music writer Craig Jenkins acknowledges that drug and alcohol abuse has always featured in hip hop, as it has in rock, country, EDM, and virtually every other genre of popular music. But Jenkins hears something new in how trap music deals with substance abuse: "In the past, rhymes about smoking blunts and drinking liquor were about taking a temporary vacation from yourself," whereas "the new drug rap asks why sobriety deserves to be the default setting." In trap music, drugs no longer represent a vacation but a permanent escape. Scholar Kemi Adeyemi argues that the stoned sound and lyrical content of trap music reflects the coping mechanisms used by besieged black communities, since "drugs are seen to generate productively intoxicated states that counter the violent realities of a particularly black everyday life."

The power of "Swimming Pools" lies in its acknowledgment of this violent reality and the strategies of self-medication necessary to survive it. The intense syncopation of the trap hats in the chorus, Lamar's triplet flow in the second verse, and the multiple temporal layers in the song together create seductive rhythmic textures that provide escape for the body and brain. Psychiatrists have used the song to illustrate the neural networks that govern addiction, analyzing the tracks "as a conflict between the reward and pleasure pathway of the character's mesolimbic system . . . and the executive functioning of his prefrontal cortex . . . which warns him of the dangers of getting intoxicated." What makes "Swimming Pools" even more provocative is that by song's end, it is not clear that Lamar's prefrontal cortex can overcome his mesolimbic instincts. The overwhelming pleasure of the song's syncopation can twist its message from one of caution to one of hedonism.

Indeed, its sensuality is so alluring that, contrary to Lamar's warning, "Swimming Pools" has become a pro-drinking song among college students who hear its warnings about the deep dive into inebriation as invitations. "Swimming Pools" serves both as a critique of addiction and as a testament to how compelling an escape from sobriety can be. Lamar expresses this duality through syncopation and temporal dissociation, creating sensory pleasures for listeners akin to a high. Unlike real drink and drugs, however, the beautiful thing about music is that the high of trap hats and triplet flows comes with no side effects. We can dive in and never get wet.

Music Takes You Higher

Modulation: Beyoncé—"Love on Top"

When we hear "Love on Top" (2011), its retro synthesizers and R&B harmonies transport us to the cusp of the 1990s. If the song conjures memories of Whitney Houston's soaring vocals, that's probably not an accident. Houston is one of Beyoncé's icons: "I remember meeting Whitney for the first time when I was 15. . . [S]he was the ultimate legend. The ultimate woman." Since then, Beyoncé has become a legend in her own right, known as one of the hardest-working performers in pop music. She has won twenty-two Grammy awards and joined the ranks of the best-selling musicians of all time. She has fended off declining record sales by pioneering spectacular new release formats: video albums (*Beyoncé*, 2013), surprise albums (*Lemonade*, 2016), and collaborative albums with her spouse, Jay Z (*Everything Is Love*, 2018). She has powerfully demonstrated that black feminism and pop success are not mutually exclusive. And she is revered by her loyal fans, the Beyhive, who address her by the royal epithet "Queen Bey."

"Love on Top" performed by Beyoncé, written by Beyoncé Knowles, Terius Nash, Shea Taylor, Columbia Records, 2011.

In all her success, though, Beyoncé never forgot her roots, and one of her biggest hits builds on the legacy of Whitney Houston. "Love on Top" and other songs that reference past musical styles can capture the attention of both teenagers, pop's target audience, and older generations wistful for the music of their youth. Research into music cognition shows that we form the strongest attachment to music we listen to as teenagers. Appeals to nostalgia reach a larger audience and therefore sell more records. Beyoncé is far from alone in using this tactic. The prince of nostalgia, Bruno Mars, has industrialized the practice. "Locked Out of Heaven" (2012) looks back to the Police's "Roxanne" (1978), "Uptown Funk" (2014) contains a smorgasbord of '70s references, and "24K Magic" (2016) emulates the '80s electro-funk of Roger Troutman and Zapp. Go to one of Mars's concerts, and you're likely to witness countless parents shamelessly dancing alongside their mortified teenage children.

In the 2010s, the sounds of the late '80s and early '90s swept across the Billboard charts. Quick on the draw, Mars released "Finesse (Remix)" featuring Cardi B (2018), which looks back to the sound of new jack swing —the beat is a subtly reengineered rhythm from Bell Biv Devoe's "Poison" (1990). The new jack swing style, crafted by Teddy Riley and popularized by Janet Jackson, dominated the '90s with hits like Montell Jordan's "This Is How We Do It" (1995). Composing an effective contemporary song that embodies the sounds of the past is a significant challenge, one Mars meets with distinction. But well before Mars, Beyoncé resurrected the distinctive sounds of the period with "Love on Top." More than an homage, "Love on Top" exploits classic pop sounds and techniques to increase the song's power and depth.

Written by Beyoncé, Shea Taylor, and Terius "The-Dream" Nash, "Love on Top" is constructed around an uplifting message of love. The song follows Beyoncé as she reflects on the power of her partnership. Its beginning is subdued, finding Beyoncé in a contemplative mood, reflecting on how far her relationship has come. We can hear the joy in her voice, as she's "smiling out from ear to ear." Moving into the pre-chorus, the lyrics reveal a discordant past of tears and hurt. For Beyoncé, traveling through these difficult moments makes her sustained relationship that much sweeter, and in the chorus she discloses that the source of her joy is her lover choosing to prioritize her over all else: finally, he's put her "love on top." The song builds over the course of each section, mimicking her ever-more elated state. The music becomes increasingly transcendent, topping itself by adding lively instrumentation into each section: synths sparkle in the verse, backing vocals join the pre-chorus, horns stab in the chorus, and diva-like vocals rise higher and higher during the extended outro.

Just as Beyoncé looks back on her relationship, the timbres of "Love on Top" look back to her musical forebears, recreating the textures of 1980s and 1990s R&B. From its first chord, "Love on Top" locates itself in the past. We hear the naked electric piano preset of a Yamaha DX7 playing a bright and cheery G major chord. This digital synthesizer was ubiquitous in hits of the 1980s and '90s, including Whitney Houston ballads like "Greatest Love of All" (1986), "I Will Always Love You" (1992), and "I Have Nothing" (1993). Over this digital piano, a chorus of guitars plays in unison as Beyoncé scats "ba-da-ba-da." Then a synthesized bass fills the lower register, outlining a syncopated rhythm that dances around the carefree vocal. It's the same bass synthesizer sound heard on countless Teddy Riley productions of the 1990s. Only three measures into "Love on Top," we are set firmly in the past, and the drums haven't even entered yet. Beyoncé then directs the rhythm section to "bring the beat in!" The snare drum is instantly recognizable with its long reverberant tail. Each time the snare hits, its resonating *snap* sounds as if it's filling an empty museum, bouncing down the gallery halls. This explosive effect is fundamental to '80s pop and '90s R&B. Together the digital electric piano, funk bass, and reverberant snares all conjure the recent pop past.

The song's nostalgic timbres are reinforced by its chord progression; "Love on Top" lifts its chromatic harmonies directly from New Edition's "Mr. Telephone Man" (1984), probably the only song ever written about a technical support call. One of R&B's great contributions to popular music is its expanded harmonic vocabulary. In Chapter 3 we saw how "We Are Young" uses tonal harmony to tug our ear between the duality of home and away, using a limited set of familiar chords—the equivalent of coloring with an eight-count box of crayons. R&B introduces chromaticism into its harmonies, using notes that sit outside the safety of the song's key. Chromaticism gives songwriters a larger palette of chords, each with their own subtleties and emotional effect—like graduating to the jumbo crayon box, the one with sixty-four different colors. R&B is not the only style to use chromaticism; it's been ubiquitous throughout music history. J.S. Bach ornamented his Baroque choral pieces with chromaticism. Clara Schumann's chromatic palette lent her piano works psychological depth in the Romantic era. Etta James used chromatic slides in "At Last" (1960) to impart a bluesy quality— Beyoncé even cites James as her influence for "Love on Top," having played the singer in the film *Cadillac Records* (2008). In "Love on Top," the chromatic harmonies adhere firmly to a '90s R&B aesthetic by borrowing those from "Mr. Telephone Man." But a chord progression isn't the only thing Beyoncé borrows from New Edition—"Love on Top" also adopts the group's visual aesthetic. The "Love on Top" video directly references New Edition's video for "If It Isn't Love" (1988). Both are staged in a sunlit urban loft and feature a boy band dressed in urban street wear performing synchronized dance moves. Combined with the throwback timbres and chromatic harmonies, this visual identity imbues "Love on Top" with retro nostalgia.

"Love on Top" does more than borrow the timbres, chromaticism, and clothing of its R&B influences. It also employs a musical technique that is rarely used today but was common in the late 1980s and early '90s: **modulation**. A modulation occurs when a composer changes the home key of the song, something that can be more of a felt experience than a conscious one. When we experience a musical lift or an abrupt departure, often it's due to modulation. In the era of new jack swing, musicians loved to modulate, especially upwards, towards the end of a track. On an episode of Switched On Pop, songwriter Dru Cutler uses the metaphor of an apartment building to illuminate the power of each key and to simplify the concept of modulation:

> Imagine you live in a twelve story apartment building with one unit per story—luxurious, we know. Instead of door numbers, each apartment is assigned a letter. Because the building contractor messed up the lettering, the seven west facing apartments run C, D, E, F, G, A, B. The five apartments on the east add a ♯ symbol: C♯, D♯, F♯, G♯, A♯ [Figure 10.1]. You live in apartment C. You like your apartment. It's nicely decorated. One night, sitting on your sofa munching on chips, you are flicking through the TV channels and can find nothing to watch. So you see if your neighbor wants to hang out. You get up, walk up the stairs to the next unit, and knock on apartment C♯. Your neighbor greets you and you go inside. Even though the layout is the same, your friend's apartment has its own feel and decor. It's almost identical, but at the same time refreshingly different and a welcome change from a night spent bored on the sofa. The two of you decide to bake cookies, but realize you are out of sugar. So you get up and walk all the way upstairs to your friend in apartment B, on the highest floor. Again, B is laid out just like your apartment

FIGURE 10.1 Musical keys as ascending units in an apartment building.

C, but this one is brighter and is plastered with cheery wallpaper. You all bake cookies, and hand them out to the rest of your neighbors whose apartments are just like yours, only on different floors and with subtle design differences.

Musical keys are much like this apartment building. Each one sounds more or less the same. The major scale in C sounds like a major scale in D, except that in D all the notes are audibly higher, though in the same relative position. When an artist modulates up a key, the experiential lift comes from the same order of notes being played higher up. So, does it matter which key you start in? For some musicians, keys display distinct qualities. For the ancient Greeks some keys evoked war and others peace. Baroque composer Marc-Antoine Charpentier assigned subjective emotional qualities to each key. For Charpentier, C Major sounded "gay and warlike," while E♭ major sounded "cruel and severe." Some people with synesthesia associate keys with colors, hearing keys in black, pink, purple, or red. Beyond their subjective qualities, the right key can enhance the sound of a solo instrument. Violin concertos are predominantly written in keys that allow the violinist to take advantage of the resonant open strings on the instrument. Many hip hop and EDM tracks use the keys of F and F♯ because they approach the lowest audible bass note that can be reliably produced on a club's subwoofer. But most often, pop performers choose a key that is comfortable and fits their voice best, not too low or too high.

In the outro of "Love on Top," Beyoncé modulates into higher and higher keys, showing off the range of her voice (Figure 10.2). At the end of the second post-chorus, just after Beyoncé sings "you put my love on top, top, top, top, top," the song rises from C up to C#, giving Beyoncé a higher key to belt out her melody (3:07). In the music video, the lights dim to night and spotlight the dancers, who've changed from streetwear into '70s silver disco suits (note that the edit for the video is a minute shorter than the recording, so the timestamps don't align). The chorus repeats, this time abbreviated without a post-chorus. Singing another key higher, Beyoncé repeats "you put my love on top." As if taking her direction, the song moves up yet one more key— to D. On cue, Beyoncé and her backup dancers change costumes again, this time dressed in Motown-era bow ties—her finicky time machine seems to run backward each time the song moves

FIGURE 10.2 Beyoncé modulating the chorus upward from C, to C♯, to D, to D♯ to E.

upward. Twice more the song floats upward, and the dancers end up in Fred Astaire top hats from the 1920s, Beyoncé in Ginger Rogers tights with a sequined, penguin tail jacket. Each modulation nods deeper into the past while traveling further up Beyoncé's vocal range. We call this progressive, upward key change a **diva modulation**, as it demands extreme vocal acrobatics.

A diva modulation, named for those female singers with extraordinary voices and personas to match, is any upward key change, usually stepwise, that allows the diva to reach new sonic heights. Though diva modulations are less common in contemporary pop, a careful listener would have noticed at least two moments of foreshadowing earlier in the song. First, the Whitney Houston–style electric keyboard from the intro is a significant spoiler. Whitney Houston was the queen of modulations. Her most iconic example, "I Will Always Love You" (1992), sends shivers down our spines even after countless listens. Leading into Houston's final chorus at 3:08, the key modulates up a whole step, raising the stakes of her love and giving Houston the chance to show off her diva range. Like Houston, Beyoncé saves her modulations for the end of the song, working up to them for three whole minutes.

But before Beyoncé takes us to the climax, she teases us in the pre-chorus. In the second half of the first chorus (1:21), Beyoncé grabs the listener by the lapel: "When I need to make everything stop." Right on the word "stop," all of the music cuts out. She has our attention. This example of clichéd text painting (Chapter 6), where her lyric commands the music to literally stop, suits the moment. The stop is a setup for the song's thesis. Beyoncé breaks the silence with her refrain "finally you put my love on top." But she doesn't stop there, she continues to raise the bar at 1:26: "you put my love on top, top, top, top, top" (Figure 10.3). Each time she sings top, she moves stepwise up the scale, so that each top comes higher than the one before it (with a final dip at the end). The melodic text painting prefigures the diva modulations to come.

Beyond just showing off her vocal prowess, "Love on Top" practically instructs Beyoncé to modulate into a higher key— the song needs to fulfill the promise of its title. By connecting the song's message to its modulation technique, "Love on Top" exposes another form of key change: the **narrative modulation**.

FIGURE 10.3 Beyoncé's melody rises up the scale each time she sings "top" during the first chorus, at 1:26.

While the diva modulation showcases a singer's ability style, the narrative modulation is used to support the dramatic arc of a song. Once again, Beyoncé follows the lead of Whitney Houston, who uses a narrative modulation in another one of her hits, "I Wanna Dance with Somebody" (1987). At 3:06, Houston sings a plaintive lyrics: "When the night falls/My loneliness calls." Then, as if in defiance of the falling night and her deepening solitude, Houston raises the entire key of the song up a step, launching into the final chorus at 3:11 with the confident announcement, "Oh, I wanna dance with somebody." Here, the modulation supports the song's lyrical journey. Beyoncé uses the same technique in "Love on Top," enhancing the narrative of her growing love by elevating the harmony ever-upward. This is the genius of "Love on Top"—its modulations are of both the *diva* and the *narrative* variety. By combining the two, showcasing her vocal virtuosity while drawing listeners into the song's message, Beyoncé ensures that the song will be unforgettable.

In 2011, most Billboard hits drew their sounds primarily from EDM, making "Love on Top" a retro sonic standout. But Beyoncé proves that sounds from the past are viable in the present, if delivered in a compelling way. And the payoff in "Love on Top" is sensational. Where other singers might tap out, Beyoncé rises higher, showing off her exceptional vocal abilities in a joyful celebration of love. Her ascending voice echoes the ceaseless ascent of her celebrity. As the song fades out, we are left wondering, "How high can she possibly go?" Will Beyoncé top herself yet again?

The Performance of Identity

Counterpoint: Britney Spears— "Oops! . . . I Did It Again"

At the turn of the twenty-first century, Britney Spears was everywhere. One of the most exposed figures of the time, her every move was dissected and discussed ad nauseum by a ravenous media. Yet somehow, Spears remained an enigma. Her celebrity hinged on dizzying contradictions: Southern Christian values and sexual liberation; conservative politics and a huge gay fan base; virginal purity and licentiousness. Everyone wanted to know, "Who is Britney Spears?" Was she a role model or an example of everything wrong in the world?

We may never learn the answer. Spears's musical output reinforces her unknowable public persona, an integral part of her performed identity. To perform one's identity is to enact a particular, intentional public face—the clothes we wear, the expressions we use, or in the case of a pop star, the music we make. But that doesn't mean identities can't change. As the cultural theorist Stuart Hall has argued, "Instead of thinking of identity as an already accomplished fact . . . we should think,

"Oops!...I Did it Again" performed by Britney Spears, written by Max Martin, Rami Yacoub, Jive Records, 2000.

instead, of identity as a 'production,' which is never complete, always in process." None of us is only one thing, and our identities are in constant flux, adjusting to our circumstances and to the need to fit in or represent ourselves as we want to be perceived. In Spears's music, she exposes this plastic nature of identity. The lyrics of her 2001 hit, "I'm Not a Girl, Not Yet a Woman," for example, capture the blend of guilelessness and worldliness that so fascinated Spears's fans.

But how does the music itself function in obscuring the "real" Spears from her public avatar? "Oops! . . . I Did it Again" (2000) makes an ideal track for exploring the specifically *musical* construction of identity. Composed by Max Martin and Rami Yacoub, "Oops!" has been recognized as a near-perfect pop masterpiece. But in large part because of Spears's perceived lack of "authenticity," the song was met with critical rejection on its release. The Los Angeles Times dismissed "Oops!" as "hollow and fake," appealing only to young ears, since "Spears's sophomore collection has all the brass and burble millennial adolescents expect from their ear candy. More jaded listeners will hear the same slick soul-pop, metronomic beats and overwrought balladry as before, but, really, who cares what they think?" The fiercest invective came from the *AV Club*, in a blistering critique worth quoting in full:

> Processed, airbrushed, (allegedly) augmented, and bleached of anything resembling charisma, Spears is a true cipher, a dress-up doll programmed to satisfy as many different fans and fantasies as possible. So it's no surprise that . . . "Oops! . . . I Did It Again" is a joyless bit of redundant, obvious, competent cheese, recycling itself at every turn and soliciting songwriting from . . . soulless hacks . . . and assorted Swedes.

What did these critics want from Spears? At the turn of the millennium, Britney Spears embodied what music journalist Ann Powers describes as "a seismic shift in American culture—not toward the cultivated rawness of rock and roll, but away from it, into an era dominated by new technologies that throw into question the very nature of the authentic." Highbrow music publications approached Spears and Martin's creations with a mixture of suspicion and derision—often laced with language of sexism and ageism—and failed to recognize that Spears represented a new kind of pop star. Unlike Joni Mitchell, or Bob Dylan, or other rock icons lauded by critics of an earlier generation, Spears was not a singer-songwriter transforming her innermost emotion and personal experience into musical expression. She was in fact just what the *AV Club* reviewer attests—a cipher, a mirror for our collective desires and anxieties. When writer Chuck Klosterman interviewed Spears in 2003, he found her performed persona equally disarming and brilliant, since "as long as she never dictates her character—as long as Spears never overtly says 'This is who I am'—everyone gets to inject their own meaning. Subconsciously, we all get to rebrand Britney Spears."

Spears's anti-authenticity was a response to a pop industry reeling from the rise of Napster and the resulting precipitous decline in the earning power of music. The eponymous album on which "Oops!" appeared was one of the last records to sell more than 20 million copies. During the 1990s, twenty-two albums hit that mark. Since 2000, there have been only four: Norah Jones's *Come Away with Me* (2002); Usher's *Confessions* (2004); and Adele's *21* (2011) and *25* (2015). In the post-Napster era, pop stars could no longer rely on album sales to generate income. They had to transform themselves into what communications scholar Leslie M. Meier calls "artist-brands." In the twenty-first century, pop artists have to sell themselves—the more an artist's brand refracts and engages different identities, the more the artist can command attention and profits. For some, the celebrity-first music economy may be creatively stifling. For Jay Z it provides both lyrical inspiration and an investment opportunity: "I'm not a businessman; I'm a business, man!" But either way, if you're an aspiring pop star, mass marketing your image is non-optional. In this light, the *A.V. Club*'s withering review of "Oops!" says more about its author's perspective than Spears's merit as a musician. Rather than seeing in Spears a "dress-up doll programmed to satisfy as many different fans and fantasies as possible," we find an ingenious artist-brand designed to generate controversy and confrontation. Rather than hearing in "Oops!" a "joyless" tune composed by "soulless hacks . . . and assorted Swedes," we recognize an accomplished work of timbral variation, harmonic ambiguity, and contrapuntal daring, devised by "an assorted Swede" who would become one of the most successful songwriters of our time.

"Oops!" illustrates how Spears keeps listeners an ear's-length away from her "real" self, because every musical element in the track explodes the very notion of the singer having any "real" self at all. The contradictions begin in the chorus with the childlike "Oops . . . I did it again," followed by the claim, "I'm not that innocent." Which is it? The music provides no answers. Spears's vocal timbre alternates between knowing maturity and naïve wonder; the harmonic progression in the chorus waffles between major and minor; and in the piece's masterstroke, the final chorus launches into **counterpoint**, an age-old technique in which separate melodies are sung against each other.

Like Sia, Kendrick Lamar, and many of the most successful pop stars, Spears's vocal timbre is an essential marker of her identity. We hear her unmistakable tone at the start of "Oops!" in the form of a wordless exhortation: "Yeah yeah yeah yeah yeah." The huskiness in Spears's voice communicates deep world weariness. When the first verse starts at :20, she switches up her timbre to a more childish sound, focusing on higher vocal frequencies with delicate, lilting melismas on words like "crush." When the chorus hits at :50, Spears delivers a third, intermediate timbral variation, somewhere between the husky "yeah yeahs" of the song's intro and the childish naiveté of the verse. In the chorus, her timbre is steady and confident, buoyed by a choir of backup vocals. Then in the second verse, her childlike tone returns. Bouncing between maturity and innocence, Spears keep us guessing which is the "true" Britney, effortlessly performing either identity through skillful timbral variation.

Another element that keeps us from penetrating the psyche of Britney Spears is the carefully constructed harmonic progression of the song's chorus. Switching back and forth between major and minor chords, the harmonies can't decide which tonality to settle on. The first line, "Oops, I did it again/I played with your heart," is set to minor harmonies. Right on the word "heart," the song's chords switch to major. The next line, "got lost in the game," continues in major, then transitions back to minor under the lyrics "oh baby, baby." Chorus after chorus, the chords cycle from minor to major and back, keeping listeners uncertain about the tonal home of the piece, just as they are uncertain about the true nature of Spears. Harmonic ambiguity in "Oops" acts as an effective metaphor for the post-authentic qualities of millennial pop, but the chorus's chord progression is far from new. As explored in Chapter 3, certain harmonic progressions have long histories of use. Of all the archetypal chord progressions that have scaffolded popular music, the one used in "Oops!" stretches back further than any other. "La Folia" is a set of chord changes first documented in the seventeenth century, but scholars think it can be traced back to the Middle Ages. The eighteenth century found Handel and Vivaldi picking up the "Folia" chord progression, as did Franz Liszt in the nineteenth century and Sergei Rachmaninoff in the twentieth. Max Martin, Rami Yacoub, and

Britney Spears thus represent twenty-first practitioners of an ancient musical code, using it to craft a song that projects distinctly modern dualities.

The crowning, confounding moment of "Oops!" arrives toward the end of the song, after Spears has growled and purred her way through two verses, two choruses, and a delightfully dated bridge section that references the doomed romance in the film *Titanic* (1998). Then, at 2:29, something surprising occurs. The song seems to return to the chorus, but it's not the same chorus we have heard before. While the original chorus started on the downbeat, this altered version shifts the lyric "Oops" to the second beat of the measure. The lyrics are also varied slightly, from "Oops, I did it again/*I played with your heart*/Got lost in the game" to "Oops, I did it again/*To your heart*/Got lost in *this* game." The melody unfolds differently as well, holding to the general contour of the original chorus but landing on alternate pitches. The overall effect gives listeners something new yet recognizable at once, creating musical variation while still delivering the song's most familiar section.

After the alternate chorus, Spears, Martin, and Yacoub return to a statement of the original chorus. At this point, most listeners would expect the song to end, or perhaps to repeat another chorus. Instead, we get something utterly unexpected— an eruption of counterpoint. Spears sings the alternate chorus and the original chorus *at the same time*. Music theorist Megan Lavengood dubs this maneuver "the cumulative chorus," recognizing that the slight and seemingly arbitrary variations in the alternate chorus turn out to have been deliberately chosen to contrast with the original chorus. When the melodies of the alternate and original chorus are stacked on top of one another, each pitch either fits into the gaps or harmonizes in perfect counterpoint with its complement. Figure 11.1 visualizes the careful balance of the "cumulative chorus" by layering the original chorus (top/capitalized) over the alternate chorus (middle/cursive); and showing how they work in tandem in the final, cumulative chorus (bottom panel).

The use of counterpoint in the final chorus of "Oops!" lends the song its most triumphant and illusory moment. From the Renaissance through the eighteenth century, counterpoint was favored by Western composers from Josquin to Bach and Handel. The more complicated the melody, or the more melodies that were stacked up, the more difficult the exercise became. Bach's famous *Art of the Fugue*, left incomplete at the end of his life, is perhaps the most exhaustive exercise in contrapuntal possibilities and experimentation in music literature. If Bach and company were drawn to counterpoint to test their compositional skill, listeners were drawn to counterpoint because of the powerful effect of multiple realities sounding together.

Counterpoint represents one of music's unique artistic properties. The human brain is unable to comprehend numerous

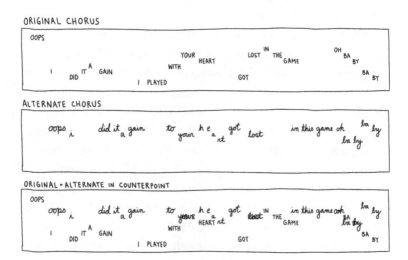

FIGURE 11.1 Original chorus, alternate chorus, and cumulative chorus in counterpoint with each other.

monologues at once—something you can test by taking the middle seat on a plane and trying to eavesdrop simultaneously on the people sitting on either side of, in front of, and behind you. We can only comprehend one speaking voice at a time, and we tune the others out in order to do so. Melody is a different game, however. When Spears sings the alternate chorus and the original chorus at the end of "Oops!," we not only hear each individual melody but we also hear a third part: the new melody created by combining the two. Similar to the way that Kendrick Lamar creates multiple rhythmic subdivisions at once in "Swimming Pools" (see Chapter 9), Spears sings multiple melodies, making it impossible to determine which is the "true" melody. We cannot focus on just one melody; we can only hear them in the aggregate. This is an effective metaphor for identity itself, since the elements that make up our identities may be indivisible, but we are always greater than the sum of their parts.

Timbral variation, harmonic ambiguity, and a cumulative, contrapuntal final chorus all work together to make "Oops!" a masterwork of muddled identity. Each compositional technique distances us from the "real" Spears, even as we are reeled deeper into the song's pleasures. Vexed by such techniques, critics took aim at "the man behind the curtain," Max Martin. When "Oops!" was released, Martin was dismissed by the media as a "soulless hack," one of the "assorted Swedes" invading the American pop industry, likely because Martin seemed to represent the depersonalization and industrialization of modern pop. That a mysterious foreigner lurked behind the biggest American hits of the moment was surely unsettling to many who prize authenticity from their pop stars. But in contrast to classical music or rock, according to musicologist Susan McClary, pop music has always been the "result of complex collaborative processes." While Clara Schumann is attributed as the sole composer of her Piano

Trio in G Minor, opus 17 (1846), when it comes to pop, "there is no single originary genius"; rather, an artist is "best understood as the head of a corporation that produces images of her self-representation, rather than as the spontaneous, 'authentic' artist of rock mythology." Martin may thus be the ghost in the corporate machine to some, but his behind-the-scenes role has a long-standing precedent.

Martin, in fact, shares much in common with a hit-maker of a century prior. Irving Berlin was born in 1888 to a Jewish cantor in modern-day Belarus, and immigrated to the United States with his family at the age of five. Over the course of a six-decade career, Berlin penned more classic songs than can be listed here, including "White Christmas" (1942), "God Bless America" (1938), "Puttin' on the Ritz" (1929), "Cheek to Cheek" (1935), and "There's No Business Like Show Business" (1946). Berlin was a crucial player in establishing the business of producing popular songs and even started his own publishing company. In 1916, Berlin generated a series of "rules" for being an effective songwriter, many of which remain applicable over a hundred years later:

> Begin with an idea for either a title, phrase or melody, and hum it out to something definite. . . . Gather ideas. . . . [W]ork them out between eight o'clock at night and five in the morning. . . . In the next stage, words and music are worked out more fully in collaboration with another songwriter and/or an arranger. . . . Conform stylistically to the music best known to your audiences. . . . [Q]uote and parody familiar melodic material. . . . Writing melodies that are too original . . . is dangerous. . . . Set text in a predominantly syllabic fashion . . . mostly diatonic tunes confined to a range of an octave. . . . Harmonies are tonal and triadic, shaped into two- or four-bar phrases.

"Oops!" fits most of Berlin's 1916 guidelines. It is predominantly syllabic (one pitch per syllable, as opposed to using melisma), structured in two- or four-bar phrases, and has a range of just over an octave. Its musical qualities are familiar without being derivative, and the song was the product of a highly collaborative process. Though the tools have changed, Berlin's assembly-line approach to pop has proven remarkably durable.

This formulaic approach elicited backlash for its perceived lack of authentic artistry. Despite his success, Berlin, like Martin, was criticized for being a "hack" with no obvious compositional trademarks. Unlike Taylor Swift (with whom Martin has worked extensively), neither Berlin nor Martin displays a melodic signature like the "T Drop" for listeners to latch onto. There are no obvious signs to make one say, "This is clearly a Max Martin song." Still, distinct techniques like Martin's "cumulative chorus" reveal the soul operating the machinery in the song factory. Savvy listeners would have heard the cumulative chorus in a bevy of Martin-produced songs around the turn of the millennium, including Spears's "Stronger" (2000) and the Backstreet Boys' "I Want It That Way" (1999).

Martin and Spears may not be the "authentic" stars that certain music critics and fans want them to be, but authenticity is not in the nature or the formula of modern pop. For musicologist Simon Frith, what distinguishes pop from other genres is that it avoids individual emotion and is instead "designed for public use." The more mass appeal, the more success a pop song has, and that means sounding a prismatic idea of identity. The music in "Oops!" never allows listeners to locate an authentic Britney. But maybe that is okay. Better to just enjoy the ancient chord progression borrowed from "La Folia," Spears's masterful timbral variation, and Martin's clever counterpoint in the final chorus. All will live on long past our pent-up anxieties over the unanswerable question, "Who is Britney Spears?"

Is Collage a Crime?

Sampling: M.I.A.—"Paper Planes"

We were surrounded, trapped in a crowd of thousands. An air raid siren blared out emergency warnings. A figure moved up the stage wearing a peaked military hat and aviator glasses, shouting into a megaphone, "Third World Democracy!" Then a strange rendition of the Clash's "Straight to Hell" (1982) came on over the speakers, followed by three consecutive gunshots. For a moment, we thought we were witnessing a coup d'état. What we had in fact heard was Mathangi Arulpragasam, better known as M.I.A., launching into her hit single "Paper Planes" on her 2008 tour.

On first listen to "Paper Planes," it would be reasonable to believe that M.I.A. is the ruthless don of a transcontinental criminal empire: "Some I murder, some I let go." But there's another way to hear the track: as a parody that hyperbolizes immigrant stereotypes to mock the race-baiting language of criminality. Drawing from M.I.A.'s experience as a first-generation Sri Lankan in London, "Paper Planes" elaborates on her difficulty obtaining a US visa—she was put on the Homeland Security Risk List in 2006 because of political messaging in her music. It turns out the

"Paper Planes" performed by M.I.A., written by Maya Arulpragasam, Wesley Pentz, Topper Headon, Mick Jones, Paul Simonon, Joe Strummer, XL Records, 2008.

US government isn't easily persuaded by artistic subtext. In the song, her character hastily moves from counterfeiting visas (so-called paper planes), to hopping trains, to rifling cash registers, to boasting about a rap sheet longer than than the KGB. Instead of telling a heist narrative, M.I.A. weaves together a montage of criminal tropes, insisting in an interview with the *FADER* magazine that "it's up to you how you want to interpret it."

"Paper Planes" is an unlikely pop hit, combining a B-side sample from 1980s punk outfit the Clash, a children's choir, and in-your-face lyrics about drugs and money, all punctuated by the deafening sounds of cash register bells and gunshots. A collage of music and noise, the song not only cohered into an undeniably catchy dance track, but it also soared to #4 on the Billboard charts and launched M.I.A.'s career. Adorned in neon-and-gold revolutionary imagery adapted from her Tamil heritage, M.I.A. staged a musical takeover with "Paper Planes." The song stood out on the 2008 pop charts because of M.I.A.'s image and her creative use of sampled sound. Instead of crafting a melodically catchy hook, M.I.A. manipulated random and disturbing sound effects. How do you sing along to gun shots? To stand out on the charts, "Paper Planes" uses **sampling**, the technique of incorporating other sound recordings into a new composition. With its provocative sounds and political edge, "Paper Planes" has much to teach us about the art and legality of sampling in modern pop music.

Before it found its footing in pop, sampling came from a long line of technological experimentation that criss-crossed oceans and genres. In 1940s Paris, music pioneer Pierre Schaeffer experimented with sampling in a style called *musique concrète*—a musical form created by combining prerecorded sections of tape. Schaeffer created the first "loops" by splicing lengths of tapes end-to-end, allowing the sound to play continuously, and collaged fragmentary series of train recordings into one of the first pieces ever made purely from samples, "Etude aux chemins de fer" (1948). John Lennon and Yoko Ono employed the same tape-splicing technique to create the Beatles' "Revolution 9" (1968), but this highly technical form of music-making otherwise failed to catch on outside academic circles. The Fairlight CMI, introduced in 1979, was one of the first digital keyboards that could play back looped audio samples, and while it made sampling easier, the CMI didn't make the practice any more accessible. Though the device introduced the term "sampling," its $70,000 price tag made it unattainable for most artists. Its use was limited to expensive studios, though it did introduce an "orchestral hit" sample from Igor Stravinsky's *Firebird Suite* that has been used by artists from Keith Sweat to Yes to Jennifer Lopez.

The appearance of affordable digital samplers in the 1980s enabled a proliferation of sample-based music. Public Enemy assembled upward of 150 samples in their groundbreaking album *Fear of a Black Planet* (1990). The Midi Production Center, or MPC, especially expanded sampling capabilities, allowing musicians to capture any piece of audio up to thirteen seconds long and trigger it with the press of a button on a 4x4 grid. The device gave musicians an infinitely expanded palette: any recorded sound became fair game. Its inventor, Roger Linn, saw this box as more than a machine. In a video on the MPC's history, music journalist Estelle Caswell recovers one of the devices manuals in which Linn wrote, "I like to think of the MPC3000 as the piano or violin of our time." Indeed, performing samples on the MPC requires the rhythmic dexterity of a drummer and the melodic intuition of a guitar player (Figure 12.1). Its legacy is inseparable from the development of sample-based hip hop—the MPC became the musical foundation for artists like Dr. Dre or Kanye West. Its historical significance was cemented when the Smithsonian acquired producer J Dilla's MPC.

As sampling technology became widely available and accessible, legal interventions curtailed its progress as an artform.

FIGURE 12.1 An MPC sampler is an instrument just like drums or guitar.

In the landmark 1991 case *Biz Markie Grand Upright Music, Ltd. v. Warner Bros. Records Inc.*, the courts declared that sampling without permission constituted copyright infringement. To Biz Markie's great misfortune, he was unable to obtain permission to sample Gilbert O'Sullivan's "Alone Again (Naturally)" (1972) but did so anyway on his 1991 track of the same name, "Alone Again." The guilty verdict against Biz Markie would forever change music. It's also not insignificant that this ruling, aimed at a black hip hop icon, came down during the height of the '90s culture wars. In his deciding argument, Judge Kevin Duffy admonished defendant Biz Markie by invoking scripture: "Thou shalt not steal." The defendant's attorney expanded this "law and order" line of argument, arguing "Sampling is a euphemism that was developed by the music industry to mask what is obviously thievery." This ruling bucked established musical practice. For the first two decades of hip hop, it had been common practice to sample small portions of music without obtaining permission. One sample-clearing business estimated that 99 percent of drum samples were used without permission prior to 1992.

US copyright law allows for the reproduction of commercial material if the copy is sufficiently "transformative" from the original—a defense called "fair use." The fair use doctrine is broadly defined and applied differently in each art form. The photographer Richard Prince, known for pushing the boundaries of fair use, famously copied an advertisement featuring the Marlboro Man, cropped out the logo, and successfully claimed that the transformed photographs commented on American identity and commerce. But the same leniency for creative commentary does not apply to the more litigious music industry. In the 2005 case *Bridgeport Music, Inc. v. Dimension Films*, N.W.A.'s two-second sample of a Funkadelic song was deemed an infringement of Funkadelic's copyright even though it had been common practice to construct hip hop drum beats on an MPC with indiscernible slices of sound. Henceforth, all samples, no matter the length, required permission.

This is the world into which "Paper Planes" emerged. The *Biz Markie* and *Bridgeport* verdicts birthed a lucrative marketplace for copyright attorneys, publishing companies, and recording owners, in which a single sample clearance routinely sells for $10,000. Copyrights are rarely owned by the original performer, so it's often the publishing companies and record labels, not the artists, who reap the profits from sample clearance. Immediately following the court's verdict in *Bridgeport*, publisher Bridgeport Music brought over 800 copyright claims, looking to monetize their newly minted intellectual property. Maximizing corporate profit through intellectual property lawsuits has more in common with software industry patent trolls than other artforms. This high-price, disaggregated market forced hip hop creators to change how they make music—the old style of sampling had become cost prohibitive. It's estimated that Public Enemy would have lost $5 million on sample clearances for *Fear of a Black Planet*. The legacy of these changes can be heard in today's hip hop landscape. Today, only artists with deep pockets can afford to make sample-heavy albums. In such a landscape, samples act as status symbols. Jay Z's 2017 album *4:44* samples Notorious

B.I.G., Stevie Wonder, and Nina Simone. These samples show off Jay Z's luxury status just as much as his boastful lyrics in "The Story of O.J.": "I bought some artwork for one million/Two years later, that shit worth two million."

M.I.A. and her producer Diplo took aim at sampling's political history when they constructed "Paper Planes." Through a barrage of musical references and samples, "Paper Planes" both valorizes and satirizes myths about immigrant criminality: "All I want to do is [bang, bang, bang, bang] and a [gun cock], [cash register opening], and take your money." Given the litigious nature of music copyright, the sampled material in "Paper Planes" indexes perfectly the song's illicit themes. And the samples are as revolutionary as M.I.A.'s image, each carefully selected to fulfill a specific purpose in the song: The Clash's "Straight to Hell" (1982), Wreckx-N-Effects "Rump Shaker" (1992), along with the gunshots and cash registers. The effect is a unique sonic collage that draws from both the do-it-yourself radical politics of punk and the gangster imagery of hip hop.

Listening closely to each sample, we can refine "sampling" into a few narrower categories: loops, fragments, and lyrical references ("Paper Planes" doesn't sample whole tracks, though many artists do so creatively). A **loop** is any repeated excerpt of music. "Paper Planes" starts with four measures of the Clash's "Straight to Hell" that repeats until the end of the song. Though we have thus far characterized "Paper Planes" as a paragon of sampling techniques, there's one truth we've obscured: this loop, the main sample in this song, is not a sample at all. Because the original sample lacked low-end frequencies, Diplo painstakingly recreated the bass, guitar chops, kick drums, pads, and lead guitar. He explains that the Clash version didn't fit his track: "It's all replayed, by the way—it's not like a proper sample, because I wanted to take some parts away and make it a bit fatter."

Diplo may have also wanted to avoid tracking down the owner of a costly song recording license. Samples require two different permissions: one from publishing (the song's lyrics and music), and one from the actual song recording. Licensing can be both prohibitively costly and difficult to obtain, so it isn't uncommon to create replayed samples or "interpolations," re-recording a section of an original song with similar instrumentation. Even "Rappers Delight" (1979), the first mainstream hip hop single, was a re-recording of Chic's "Good Times" (1979). And a faithful interpolation is important. The "Straight to Hell" re-recording in "Paper Planes" retains sonic qualities that evoke the radical politics of '80s punk—the looseness of the kick, the lo-fi rumble of the bass, and the erratic performance of the lead guitar—while adding the low-end "fatness" Diplo wanted.

The Clash interpolation serves as more than just musical fodder. The lyrical narrative of "Paper Planes" is reinforced through this sampled material, but it requires deep digging to find the connections. M.I.A. and Diplo loop only the punky first four measures of "Straight to Hell," leaving out the song's later sections, which offer musical surprises: the sharp accents of ska-like horns and Caribbean rhythms. The horns and drums reference the revolutionary musical traditions of reggae, but the Clash contrast the genre's message of liberation with a faux-racist lyric. Singer Joe Strummer imitates a bigoted British man who blames the industrial decline of England ("railhead towns feel the steel mills rust") on recent waves of immigration ("there ain't no need for ya, go straight to hell boys"). In reality, Strummer was an ardent defender of the downtrodden and was himself born in Turkey to British parents in the foreign service. The song is a caricature of Thatcher-era conservatism.

"Paper Planes" reimagines the Clash from the perspective of the "Third World." Instead of assuming the role of the racist Brit, M.I.A. play-acts the opposite side, embodying the imagined immigrant from "Straight to Hell." The violent, drug-dealing antagonist poeticizes the magnitude of her smuggling empire: "We pack and deliver like UPS trucks." We hear the same evolution of the protagonist/antagonist in the sample. Moving from the introduction into the verse of "Paper Planes," the "Straight to Hell" loop merges with a hip hop sound: syncopated 808 drum beats disrupt the steady eighth-note punk feel. At one point. M.I.A. breaks character to reveal the satire, speaking directly to the reality of the archetypal struggling immigrant—"already going to hell, just pumping that gas"—simultaneously referencing the Clash's refrain and working-class attitude. The fever dream about international piracy is actually an ode to hardworking immigrants all over the world.

Adding detail to the cartoon criminal, "Paper Planes" adds the second kind of sample: sound **fragments** of guns and cash registers. Rather than repeat in a loop, these fragments play only when they are triggered—and violently underscore M.I.A.'s lyrics "All I want to do is [three gunshots] and a [gun cock] [cash register opening] and take your money." The disturbance places the listener in an active robbery. But these fragments do more than evoke criminality; they invite listener participation. Live in concert, thousands of participants animate the sounds with their bodies, pointing a finger like a gun, reloading with the thumb, and then snatching money from an imagined cash register, in a stadium-wide game of cops and robbers.

Of course, this orchestrated robbery is just "make believe." The song's producers can't just threaten the sample's copyright holder in a stickup; they too had to get permission to use these sounds. As instituted in the *Bridgeport* case, any sample, no matter what length, requires the owner's permission. Since any cash register will do, the "Paper Planes" fragment most likely came from a sound effects "sample pack." However, Diplo grabbed the gun samples from a more unlikely source: "Those gunshots are from [the video game] *Street Fighter*. It took two minutes to put the whole thing together." That these frightful gunshots come from a late 1980s arcade game further emphasizes the song's criminal parody. But given the song's hip hop orientations, the production would be incomplete without an old school rap reference.

Having already sampled a loop and a fragment, M.I.A. turns to the third sampling method: a **lyrical reference** to another song that further situates "Paper Planes" in the hip hop tradition. The main hook of "Paper Planes" reinterprets Wreckx-N-Effect's 1992 song "Rump Shaker," another Teddy Riley production (See "Love on Top," Chapter 10), with one of Pharrell Williams's first songwriting credits. The song's progressive production and hip hop techniques pair with a rhythmically engaging albeit objectifying message: "All I want to do is zoom-a-zoom-zoom-zoom/And a poom-poom, just shake ya rump." M.I.A. reclaims this misogynistic lyric, replacing the commands to "shake it" with gunshots. This creative reimagining both situates her music in a hip hop lineage while revising the genre's emphasis on bodily objectification.

By combining these loops, fragments, and lyrical references into a single composition, M.I.A. triggers our cultural imagination. Producer William Hutson of the hip hop group Clipping believes that these references conjure both geography and chronology: "Sampling puts you in a very specific place that evokes and metaphorizes memory." Given the brain's plasticity, memory recall can encode old memories with new meaning and events, and hearing a familiar sample in a unique context can alter the meaning of the original recording. "Paper Planes" incites listeners to reconsider their biases about immigrant women by hyperbolizing their criminal activity. Achieving this artistic vision would not be possible without the use of samples. Clipping's co-producer Jonathan Snipes explains the necessity of sampling in contemporary music:

A composition is not just notes. When a composition becomes timbre as well as notes and those timbres don't come from the predefined set of timbres that we've decided go in the orchestra, you need some way of notating those timbres and the best way to notate timbre is with a recording.

An expanded timbral language is one of sampling's greatest contributions to all music across time and genre. Beethoven would be jealous of the jarring yet physically unthreatening gunshots in "Paper Planes." In his piece *Wellington's Victory* (op. 91), a composition commemorating the Duke of Wellington's 1813 military victory over Joseph Bonaparte (older brother of Napoleon), Beethoven wished to mimic the fanfare of battle. But the timbres of the classical orchestra couldn't do the job—Beethoven instead included in his manuscript directions for musket fire and cannonade. Patrons of the symphony must have been rightly startled when real muskets cut in on the performance (thankfully, loaded with blanks). Today, "Paper Planes" gives listeners a thrilling musical heist with no fear of bodily harm other than hearing damage. The song also shows us that any sound can become an instrument in today's pop orchestra. All you need to do is sample it, and try not to infringe on someone's copyright in the process.

Shock, Awe, and Synthesis

Sound Design: Skrillex—"Scary Monsters and Nice Sprites"

Dubstep might be the most divisive genre in popular music. Reactions to it range from joy to horror, with little room left in between. The horror camp is well represented by James Murphy, leader of dance-pop outfit LCD Soundsystem, who opined that the style "makes me want to vomit. I just don't like it, it's not for me, but it's also not designed for me." As a musician with an obsession for vintage, analog synthesizers and keyboards, Murphy is at least self-aware that the deafening digital sounds of dubstep are "not for him."

Love it or hate it, outrageous timbre is the most recognizable, and most controversial, feature of dubstep, a musical subgenre of electronic dance music (EDM) designed to shock and awe. Whereas the tone of Sia's voice (Chapter 5) conveys visceral sonic markers of her identity, the synthetic timbres of dubstep synthesizers strive to be unrecognizable. As such, they're an example of a bewildering phenomenon of modern pop. Critic Ben Ratliff puts it simply: in today's music, "you often don't know

"Scary Monsters and Nice Sprites" performed by Skrillex, written by Sonny Moore, Mau5trap Records, 2010.

what you're hearing," since "sounds are running ahead of our vocabularies for describing them."

Digital technology has sped up the development of new timbres, something that used to take generations to develop. The violin, for instance, took three centuries to evolve into its current form, but today producers can synthesize a whole orchestra of original instruments in little more than the time it takes to complete an international flight—something Charlie witnessed firsthand when he ended up flying from Tokyo to Los Angeles on the same plane as Skrillex. The producer spent the whole trip composing on his computer, continuing to work on the session even after deboarding, laptop in one hand, all the way to the taxi stand. It's hard to overstate the newness of creating music from 1s and 0s. Contemporary synthesizers and sound design tools are now so powerful and portable that never-before-heard sounds are business as usual. As Murphy attests, this rate of change can be sonically perplexing. Songs have long since left behind traditional arrangements of guitar, piano, bass, and drums, leaving listeners to ask, "What are we even hearing?" Exploring a dubstep hit like "Scary Monsters and Nice Sprites" (2010) will reveal more about this polarizing genre and uncover some of the go-to tools of the modern pop producer.

"Scary Monsters and Nice Sprites" perfectly captures the pleasure and pain of our new timbral reality, because as the title suggests, it's a song constructed around the contrast of darkness ("scary monsters") and light ("nice sprites"). Skrillex uses timbral shifts to move from one emotional state to the other, employing a matrix of effects in the process: delay, phaser, flange, equalization, distortion, compression, chorus, panning, time-shifting, gates, sidechaining, pitch-shifting. All are significant, but in this chapter we'll focus in on a few that Skrillex uses to create a dichotomy between pleasing sprites and shocking monsters: **synthesis, filtering,** and **reverb**. Digital audio workstations (DAWs) like Ableton and ProTools give Skrillex and other producers the ability to create new sounds and manipulate existing ones with a few mouse clicks and keyboard taps. But it would be wrong to assume that because dubstep is created with the same tools we use to check social media, the style is less complex or musical than any others. "Scary Monsters" is an in-your-face composition generated from a thousand subtle choices. As its composer has said, "It's so cool that we're still in an era where people think that people have no talent if they make computer music. . . . [I]t shows how young it still is and how relevant it's going to be for a long time." To test Skrillex's hypothesis, we must venture into the sounds of his breakout hit and face the new head-on.

The song establishes a unique timbral vision with its first, synthesized sound. Contrary to the title, "Scary Monsters" actually begins with a verse that's firmly in the world of the "nice sprites," complete with a high-register, nice-sounding synthesizer melody. It's played by a striking instrument—buzzy and rough, yet somehow gentle—that Skrillex created using the virtual analog synthesizer Sylenth1. But he didn't create the sound from scratch. Instead, he started with a patch that comes installed with the synthesizer—a preset combination of tones designed by the Dutch developers behind Sylenth. The term "patch" is telling, connecting the digital software to its real-life predecessor, the modular synthesizer. When this device first emerged in the 1960s, it looked similar to an old-school telephone switchboard, with knobs, buttons, and dozens of sockets that would spit out different tones when properly wired with the right combination of quarter-inch patch cables. All that hardware now exists inside a digital program, making it easy to take a preset patch and then tweak its parameters until one reaches their specific, desired timbre. In Skrillex's case, he adjusts the preset patch just enough for it to become the perfect sound for his track—unfamiliar and slightly alien, but brought down to earth through its melodic grace.

Digital synthesis doesn't just allow producers to tweak computer-generated tones but also to manipulate recorded samples until they sound unrecognizable, something "Scary Monsters" takes advantage of in the pre-chorus (:27). At this point a new texture enters, one that seems, for a fleeting moment, "real." It's a voice, but one that's not quite human. Unsettlingly, it pronounces its lyrics backward, resulting in nebulous speech that might be written as "ooh yak eel tsash." Not only that, Skrillex tweaks the voice as he would a synthesizer, transforming its tone into something mechanical, choppy, and slightly unreal. Then, at :39, right before the chorus hits, he creates a clever point of contrast: a sample of an unprocessed and utterly lifelike human voice screaming, "Oh my gosh!" It's a moment that shocks listeners back into reality, and it comes with a wonderful backstory. Skrillex grabbed the exclamation from a 2008 video in which cup-stacking champion (it's a thing) Rachel Nedrow beats her personal best score, then launches into celebration. Skrillex wisely chooses to leave this vocal unadorned, exploiting Nedrow's unabashed enthusiasm to snap listeners to attention for the chorus to come.

When the chorus does hit at :41, the "scary monsters" finally emerge from the shadows, and they don't disappoint. It's a bracing moment because it makes use of one of the defining sounds of dubstep, the "wobble bass," or simply, the "wub." Anyone who made it through the verse and pre-chorus thinking "I'm not sure if this is for me" will likely head for the hills at this point. The wub is relentless, inescapable, a throbbing bass tone that seems to saturate every corner of the track. And whereas Skrillex created the "sprites" synthesizer in the verse by tweaking a preexisting patch, he built the fearsome "growl bass" of the chorus from the ground up using a process called FM synthesis. This heavy, distorted sound would go on to become one of the producer's signature techniques. Skrillex may not sing, but the growl bass effectively stands in for his voice as a marker of sonic identity—that is, until other producers figured out how to hack the same sound.

There's another important element in the distinctive "wah wah" sound of Skrillex's wobble bass, one that has a mundane-sounding name for all the scariness it's able to create. This is a filter, a digital tool that "filters out" and isolates different frequencies within the growl bass. Low-pass filters remove the higher frequencies from a tone, bringing its lower-sounding elements to the fore; high-pass filters do the opposite. These filters operate similarly to the "bass" and "treble" knobs found on a stereo (or within a music app). Each knob filters out how much of the low or high ends come through your speakers. The "wobble" of wobble bass is somewhat equivalent to quickly turning the bass and treble knobs on your stereo back and forth. By sustaining a note played by the growling synthesizer and then filtering its frequencies in and out, Skrillex doesn't have to change the bass pitch for listeners to experience the feeling of rapid oscillation. It's essentially the same thing that happens if you sing a syllable like "ohm" while alternately opening and pursing your lips. While the note you sing doesn't change, narrowing your mouth cavity filters out certain frequencies, creating a similar "wah wah" effect. So a low-tech way to create wobble bass is simply to growl out a bass tone and then rapidly open and close your mouth, a technique we recommend practicing in the privacy of one's home rather than while riding the bus or attending a wedding.

Synthesized growls and wobbly filters aren't the only tricks Skrillex uses in the chorus. Another reason the section sounds so scary is that Skrillex takes extra steps to ensure that its sounds jump out at the listener. He does so by carefully controlling the levels of reverb across the track. Reverb is a naturally occurring acoustic property that describes how sound vibrations

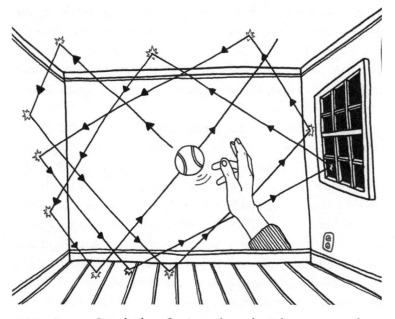

FIGURE 13.1 Reverb: the reflections of sound as it bounces around a room.

travel through a space. Imagine sound as a tennis ball. Throw one against the wall in a small room, and it will ricochet right back to you in an instant. Throw the same ball in a large space, like say, a concert hall, and it will take much longer to bounce back. Sound behaves the same way. The longer vibrations take to "bounce back" to your ear, the longer that sound will hang in the air. Small rooms thus tend to be "dead" spaces. Sing a note, and the sound will melt away almost immediately. Sing the same note in a "live" concert hall, and the sound will seem to hang in the air, sometimes for seconds (Figure 13.1).

Reverb is a subtle effect with huge import. Producers making music in computers need to add reverb to make sure their tracks don't sound completely artificial, transforming the digital vacuum into what musicologist Eric Clarke calls "virtual space." Skrillex adds digital reverb to the "nice sprites" of the verse and pre-chorus to coat the sections in warmth and depth. But when he reaches the "scary monsters" of the chorus, he dials the reverb way down. At once, the wobble bass sounds frighteningly close, with no acoustic reverb to impart virtual distance.

"Scary Monsters" has one more surprise in store. At 3:05, the processed, backward vocal from the chorus returns, singing its unintelligible "ooh yak eel tsash" refrain. But then, at 3:18, the voice suddenly flips so that it is at last singing audible words. For the first time, we can audibly hear the original lyric: "You don't need to hide my friend/For I am just like you." The reveal suggests a synthesis, if you will, between the song's disparate poles of nice sprites and scary monsters. In fact, these characters are one and the same—digital sounds generated in Skrillex's laptop. The final lyric could also be interpreted as an appeal to listeners feeling alienated by the harsh sounds of dubstep. "Don't worry," it seems to say, this genre's fans are "just like you."

It's a notion supported by studies into the psychology of sound. In 2018, a team of Australian psychologists sought to learn why some people enjoy listening to the violent sounds of death metal music while others find it grotesque. They found that non-fans associate death metal with "tension, anger and fear," while fans experience "power, joy, peace, and wonder" while listening. Dubstep shares many of the same qualities as metal: quick BPMs, loud tones, and intense rhythms—all qualities Skrillex absorbed during his early career playing in punk and hardcore bands.

Perhaps fans of dubstep derive a pleasure similar to that of metal-heads. This is something worth remembering whenever we encounter strange and alienating sounds—as James Murphy says, they may make us want to vomit, but then again, they're not *for* us, anyway. Besides, there's little point in protesting.

Timbral invention is the new normal, one of the key aspects of modern pop. Unimaginable sounds are unveiled every day. To those wishing that music sounded like the good old days, best to change the dial. But if novelty is your pleasure, you don't need to hide. All you need to do is open your ears.

Finding Home in the Harmonic Diaspora

Tonal Ambiguity: Luis Fonsi ft. Daddy Yankee—"Despacito"

Anyone with a pulse in 2017 likely heard "Despacito" by Luis Fonsi and Daddy Yankee. Everywhere one went, from the grocery store to the dentist, the plaintive Puerto Rican *cuatro* guitar followed, with a reggaetón beat and steamy lyrics right behind. The song gained traction after its release in the first weeks of January, but once Justin Bieber appeared on a remix version, its popularity exploded (this chapter's analysis uses only the original version). Earning a considerable collection of superlatives, "Despacito" was the first Spanish-language #1 song since the Bayside Boys "Macarena" in 1996, and it topped the Billboard charts for sixteen weeks—tying "One Sweet Day" (1995) by Mariah Carey and Boyz II Men as the longest running #1 song in history. With over six billion views, the music video ranks as the most-viewed ever on YouTube, and between the original recording and the Bieber remix, "Despacito" is also the most-streamed song on Spotify with over 2.2 billion plays.

"Despacito" performed by Luis Fonsi ft. Daddy Yankee, written by Luis Rodríguez, Erika Ender, Ramón Ayala, Universal Latin, 2017.

Beyond its unprecedented commercial success, "Despacito" instigated a new wave of interest in Latinx music. In 2017, three of the top five music videos played on YouTube were by Latinx artists (the other two were by Ed Sheeran). In 2018, four of the top five music videos were from Latinx artists (the other was "Girls Like You" by Maroon 5). Music writer Eduardo Cepeda sees something new in the twenty-first-century Latinx boom, a different sound and style from the mid-1990s craze that gave the public hits like "Macarena," Enrique Iglesias's "Bailamos" (1999), and Ricky Martin's "Livin' La Vida Loca" (1999). Those tracks catered to English speakers and established pop sensibilities, whereas Fonsi, Daddy Yankee, and the new generation of reggaetón artists do not "perform their Latino identities for a white lens." Instead, they give their audiences an unfiltered version of Caribbean musical culture. For critic Julianne Escobedo Shepherd, the Latinx music explosion engendered by "Despacito" has been a long time coming. At last, the Billboard charts reflect the demographic diversity of an increasingly brown nation.

What is behind the runaway success of "Despacito"? One answer is that the song's musical hybridity allows it to connect with as many listeners as possible. Longtime friends, Luis Fonsi and Daddy Yankee bring a surprising stylistic blend to the song—Fonsi built his career on slow, romantic ballads, Daddy Yankee through raw, reggaetón hits like "Gasolina" (2005). Fonsi provides a soaring, romantic vocal melody to the chorus, contrasted by the syncopated and funky flow delivered by Daddy Yankee in the second verse. By the song's outro, the two singers trade lines back and forth, weaving a compelling texture between their distinct styles.

"Despacito" also mixes new and traditional sounds of Puerto Rican music. The song begins with a plucked *cuatro* guitar, a classic element of Puerto Rican culture in use for centuries. The *cuatro*'s distinctive sound comes from five sets of paired strings that give each pluck double the resonance and force. On "Despacito" the *cuatro* is played by modern virtuoso Christian Nieves, who solos freely during the song's opening, then blends into the background of the verse and chorus sections with a supportive *tumbao* rhythm. If Nieves's expert *cuatro* playing gives "Despacito" its traditional element, the reggaetón beat that follows his opening solo pulls the track into the twenty-first century. The characteristic *dembow* rhythm of reggaetón—*booooom-ch-boom-chick, booooom-ch-boom-chick*—is instantly recognizable and endlessly engaging, with the "boom" of the bass drum sounding out a clear four-beat meter and the snare drum "chs" and "chicks" offering danceable, off-kilter syncopation.

"Despacito" pulls listeners in further with a subtle effect at the start of each chorus. Whenever Fonsi sings the titular phrase "despacito," which means "slowly" in English, the tempo of the track actually slows down. It's an ingenious bit of text painting (see Chapter 6), and it takes place only under the *first* "despacito" of each chorus, not the three iterations that follow, so listeners don't tire of the trick. As soon as Fonsi starts the word, all instrumentation drops out. His voice alone in the mix, he slows the tempo down from 89 BPM to about 70 BPM. When he reaches the "ci" of "des-pa-ci-to," the beat restarts, and the tempo picks back up to 89 BPM. If this proves difficult to hear, try tapping your finger or foot to the song's pulse a few seconds before the lyric, which first appears at 1:01. When Fonsi sings "Despacito," you will notice that your tapping becomes wildly out of sync with his lyric, only locking in once the beat returns two seconds later at 1:03. It's a blink-and-you'll-miss-it moment, one that is felt more than consciously processed, but it lures listeners deeper into the musical world of "Despacito."

Other elements we have discussed, like form and timbre, are hard at work in "Despacito," but harmony serves the most important function in the song. "Despacito" rides a chord progression that appears in modern pop music with even greater frequency than "ice cream changes" (explored in Chapter 3). The progression contains the same chords as "ice cream changes"—one minor and three major—laid out in a different order, starting on the minor chord rather than a major.

Songs ranging from Avril Lavigne's "Complicated" (2002) to OneRepublic's "Apologize" (2005) to MGMT's "Kids" (2008) all make use of this same progression, and Luis Fonsi himself reused it for his 2018 hit with Demi Lovato, "Échame la Culpa." The "Despacito" chord progression is so well-established that the only surprise is its lack of a catchy name like the "'50s progression" or "ice cream changes." Music theorist Mark Richards offers a potential moniker: the Axis progression. "Axis" in part because of the chord sequence's appearance in the 2009 video by the Australian comedy band the Axis of Awesome, in which the members perform a medley of forty-seven different songs that use the progression. Also, because of a unique property of the progression, any of its four chords can serve as the loop's starting point; thus it can be seen to rotate on an axis.

Richards notes that the Axis progression possesses a remarkable quality, one that sets it dramatically apart from its "ice cream changes" cousin. "Despacito" and other songs using the Axis chords upset the long-standing notion of a tonal "home" that we saw articulated by Jean-Philippe Rameau back in Chapter 3. Rameau's notion of tonal home shared much in common with Newton's conception of gravity, since chord progressions generate an inexorable pull back toward their tonal home. In Fun's "We Are Young," the drama of the four-chord loop consisted of leaving home, traveling to a dark, minor world, and then making one's way back to the first chord via two other major-chord steps. "Despacito" and other Axis progressions confound Rameau's notion of tonal gravity due to a core instability: it's really hard to say which chord in the progression represents the song's "true" tonal home. We tend to have a bias toward hearing the first chord in the loop as home, which in the case of "Despacito" is B minor. But there is an issue with this logic, because B minor does not always feel like home base for the song. During certain sections, the third chord in the progression, D major, exerts more tonal gravity than B minor, and the song's overall quality shifts to that of D-major-ness. One can hear this most clearly in the song's post-chorus. After each chorus, Fonsi's voice rockets up to a higher register as he sings "Quiero ver bailar tu pelo" ("I want to see your hair dance"), and he shifts to a new melody as well, one that stresses the notes of D major. After the first post-chorus, Daddy Yankee begins his verse with a melody that seems to belong back in B minor. The constant shifts between the two tonal centers are pleasantly disorienting. Between B minor and D major, which represents the "real" tonal home of the piece? (Figure 14.1).

Discussing tonal dimensions may seem esoteric, but the consequences of this progression break centuries of established musical wisdom and give contemporary pop music its own sound. That the axis chord progression in "Despacito" of B minor-G major-D major-A major exhibits two tonal homes, not one, has caused music theorists to rethink notions about tonality that have held strong for almost 300 years. Rather than gravitating toward one tonal home, pop songs using the Axis chord progression can oscillate between two. In this, they exhibit gravitational properties that would have been foreign to celestial understanding in the age of Newton and Rameau. In 1803, however, astronomer William Herschel observed a binary star: two stars rotating around one another in orbit so closely that they appear as a single luminous being to the naked eye. Today, astronomers believe that there are countless numbers of binary stars, and they offer a different metaphor through which to understand harmonic progressions. The ice cream changes in "We Are Young" could be described as moons orbiting around a

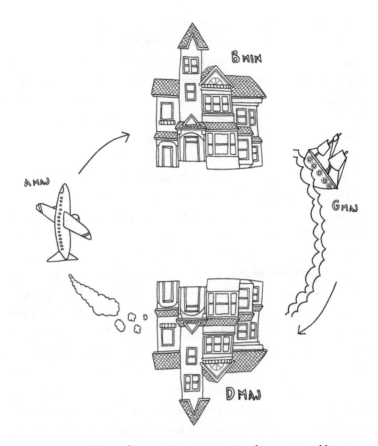

FIGURE 14.1 The ambiguous Axis progression has two tonal homes.

planet. The planet, the initial, home chord, is the most important member of the progression—all the other chords orbit around it. The Axis progression in "Despacito" is better understood as a binary star. In the Axis progression, B minor and its opposite pole, D major, present viable tonal homes. Both orbit around one another, destabilizing any harmonic hierarchy.

Richards is not the only music theorist who has investigated how the Axis progression upsets long-standing notions of tonal home. Philip Tagg proposes the concept of "tonical neighborhoods" rather than "tonal homes" to describe the progression. In Tagg's view, modern pop like "Despacito" privileges traveling over arriving. A progression like the one used in "Despacito" is "not a place you pass through en route to another destination: it's a tonical neighbourhood and is itself somewhere to be." The pleasure listeners derive from "Despacito" rests in the ambiguity of its tonal home, which keeps the song in a state of suspended animation, never quite reaching its goal.

This is especially effective because the lyrics of "Despacito" are all about reaching for, and never quite attaining, wanton lust. This is a thirsty track, one that has met its share of censure for lines in the post-chorus like "Déjame sobrepasar tus zonas de peligro/Hasta provocar tus gritos" (Let me trespass your danger zones/Until I hear you scream). The song's hedonism is exactly the point. Like so much pop music, it pushes right to the edge of social norms, and in some cases, past them. The Malaysian government banned "Despacito" from its state radio and television networks in July 2017 because of the song's perceived obscenity. The song's hypersexuality may not seem to have much to do with the harmonic ambiguity of its Axis progression, but the two are related. Both the lyrics and the harmonies in "Despacito" pose provocative ways of hearing the world.

"Despacito" not only topples notions of Rameau-ian harmony, in which every chord progression has a tonal home, but it also upsets the mythic binary that motivates so much tonal music: the idea that major and minor represent a sort of cosmic yin and yang, polar extremes of sound and emotion. In James Joyce's *Ulysses* (1922), the protagonist Leo Bloom asks himself an existential question amid a flow of stream-of-consciousness thought: "why minor sad?" It's a query worth considering. Why do the three notes of a minor triad connote sadness while the three notes of a major triad connote happiness, even though the two chords only differ by one pitch? One explanation is that connotations for major and minor are entirely cultural. In this view, only certain cultures exhibit the major/happy, minor/sad duality. It's about history and tradition more than innate qualities embedded in the chords themselves.

The other way to explain the major/minor binary is through science and cognition. Perhaps all humans are born with a synaptic link between major chords and positive emotions, minor chords and sad emotions. Music cognition scientists propose that we may be drawn to the sonic properties of a major triad because of something called the overtone series. Most sound vibrations produce multiple pitches at once. When we sing a note, we are actually singing many pitches, but most of them are so quiet that they are inaudible. You can isolate these subtle overtones if you hum a pitch with your hands over your ears. Listen closely, and there will be high, almost angelic, pitches floating over the main pitch being hummed (yes, you're humming multiple pitches at the same time!). The overtone series is important for tonality because the first two unique pitches that emerge from any overtone series create a major triad with the fundamental pitch. Every single pitch thus contains within it the full harmony of a major triad, perhaps priming us to gravitate toward the sound as something comforting and familiar. Ultimately, as with so many phenomena, our understanding of major versus minor is a mix. Not one or the other, but a combination of genetics and culture.

This duality is essential to the success of "Despacito." The song not only upsets notions of a tonal home, but it also pushes against the idea that major and minor must be diametrically opposed. In turn, this challenges the idea that major *must* be happy and minor *must* be sad. Such distinctions have consequences for the role that pop plays in society. In 2012, for instance, a study showed that pop music had increasingly used minor keys over the course of the preceding half-century. The data suggested that in the late 1960s, 85 percent of hits were in major keys, whereas in the late 2000s, only 42.5 percent were in a "happy" key. The *Washington Post* published an article on the study with the headline, "Pop Music Is Getting Sadder and Sadder," and other mainstream news outlets wrung their hands over how to parse the wider implications of a such a dark turn.

"Despacito" allows us to question such claims. First, can we even say that a song like "Despacito" is definitively either major or minor? Next, is it fair to assume that minor-key songs always connote sadness? As Talking Heads frontman David Byrne has observed, the association is a relatively recent development. "Prior to the Renaissance in Europe," Byrne asserts, "there was no connection between sadness and minor keys—implying that cultural factors can override what might be weak, though real, biological correlations." Byrne's claim is corroborated by all the pop songs that have used minor keys for joyous, celebratory purposes—songs like Rodgers and Hammerstein's "My Favorite Things" (1959), Nina Simone's "Feeling Good" (1965), and the Weeknd's "Earned It" (2014). Further, there is no shortage of major-key songs that deliver profound pathos: Hank Williams' "I'm So Lonesome I Could Cry" (1949), Radiohead's "Creep" (1993), and Rihanna and Mykki Ekko's "Stay" (2012). Whether cultural or cognitive, perhaps we make too much of the distinction between major and minor. Later in his stream-of-consciousness monologue from Ulysses, Leo Bloom returns to the question of "why minor sad?" His conclusion? "Too poetical that about the sad. Music did that. Music hath charms."

Following Bloom's lead, we would do well to be wary of accepting received wisdom about harmony. "Despacito" is the perfect song to disrupt deep-seated notions of harmonic home and major/minor binaries because it is a such a thoroughly hybridized, modern pop song. The blurriness of the song's tonal home equates to the blurred borders of our globalized world.

Pop music, like people, migrates. It is *mestizo*. As scholar Wayne Marshall points out, the genre of reggaetón itself, though associated with Puerto Rico, is thoroughly diasporic. Marshall hears in Daddy Yankee's flow equal parts Puerto Rican salsa, Jamaican dancehall, and New York hip hop. In turn, the peripatetic journeys of the song's composers and producers map to the restless harmonies in "Despacito." Luis Fonsi was born in Puerto Rico, raised in Orlando, and resides in Miami. Cowriter Erika Ender also lives in Miami, though she was born in Panama City. Producers Andres Torres and Mauricio Rengifo grew up in Colombia before relocating to Los Angeles. The migratory experiences of "Despacito's" creators are mirrored in the sound and style of the song itself. It is music for a more expansive America, one that stretches across national borders and embraces multiple homes for its diasporic communities. "Despacito" hybridizes musical geographies, time periods, instruments, styles, languages, all in the service of an unabashed ode to bodily pleasure. Small wonder it's become the most successful pop song of the twenty-first century.

Does Pop Have a Sound?

Genre: Kelly Clarkson—"Since U Been Gone"

Both pop fans and pop haters have at least one thing in common: they can immediately identify a pop song as "pop." So does this mean there is a clearly definable "pop sound"? Dumbfoundingly, there isn't. Rather, pop seems to slide fluidly across disjunct genres: new jack swing, neo soul, g-funk, reggaetón, dancehall, and mumble-rap. Pop's stylistic inconsistency refutes the idea that there is a singular pop "sound." Although niche genres like power pop, euro pop, and bubblegum pop have subsumed the word "pop," these styles don't represent the whole of popular music. That's because pop isn't a genre; it's a marketing category that encompasses everything that is commercially successful, regardless of sound. Saxophones, drum machines, sleigh bells, and synthesizers can all co-exist on the Billboard Hot 100 as long as they have a mass of listeners that drives radio play, streams, and online video—all of which count toward a song's popular ranking. Despite age-old criticism that pop is formulaic, the trending sound of the moment is rather

"Since U Been Gone," performed by Kelly Clarkson, written by Max Martin, Lukasz Gottwald, RCA Recods, 2004.

transient; genres like nu-metal, swing revival, grunge, and acid-house all came and went. The only thing reliable about pop music is the certainty that it will change. Pop is rather slippery, but perhaps we can pin it down through a case study of a songwriter who transcends stylistic boundaries and effortlessly appropriates other genres into pop—Max Martin. Martin's work on Kelly Clarkson's 2004 hit "Since U Been Gone," an indie-pop hybrid, demonstrates that while pop may not have a sound, it may have other formulaic elements. Instead of a single "pop sound," pop songs conform to certain standards like lyrical subjects, production techniques, and song forms, which work together to maximize their listenership and profitability.

Martin, the famously reclusive Swedish songwriter, needed "Since U Been Gone" to be a hit. Martin dominated the charts with R&B inspired tracks for NSYNC, Robyn, the Backstreet Boys, and Britney Spears, but had lost some of his mojo by 2004. Throwing out the formulas of '90s pop music, such as lush harmonies and synthesized drums, indie bands like the White Stripes and the Hives broke into the pop charts with guitar-driven power chords and garage rock drumming. Martin had built his career on a particular sound, which by the mid-2000s had become predictable, dated, and overproduced. But then he changed directions, spotted the growing wave of indie rock, and turned it mainstream.

Kelly Clarkson's "Since U Been Gone" is now pop canon, but it owes its success to the indie sleeper hit "Maps" by the Yeah Yeah Yeahs. When Martin first heard "Maps" he recognized its potential for mass appeal, but found it was missing a pop hook. Just when the song should explode into a climactic chorus, songwriter and singer Karen O descends into a low register, drops the energy, and effectively kills the song's momentum. Motivated to "fix" the track, Martin and co-writer Lukasz Gottwald reimagined the song with newly minted American Idol winner Clarkson behind the mic. Borrowing the breakup narrative, melodic motifs, guitar riffs, and drum rhythms from the Yeah Yeah Yeahs, Clarkson, Martin, and company crafted a #1 hit and transformed its sound into pop music. "Since U Been Gone" has been certified double platinum by the Recording Industry Association of America (RIAA). "Maps" never crossed over from Billboard's alternative charts. Why? A close listen to the music illuminates what makes one a multi-platinum success and the other an indie darling.

The similarities and differences between these songs are akin to high school social cliques. From a distance, we could say that both songs attend the same school (the key of G), take the same classes (verse-chorus form), and eat in the same cafeteria (the metaphor breaks down here). But if they did eat in the same cafeteria, they would not sit at the same table. "Maps" would be the alternative kid in the corner, scribbling poetry for the open mic. "Since U Been Gone" would be at the center table, commanding her circle of popular kids. Which is not to judge either group—they share a common objective: to create an identity that can survive the competitive high school landscape. But their approaches to high school survival could not be more different. The indie student's disdain for conformity comes through in her idiosyncratic style. Each indie kid, like each indie band, strives for his or her own unique identity. But the popular kid, like popular songs, aspires to be mainstream, attracted to the security, privilege, and successes promised by normative culture. However, these groups do not exist in isolation. The popular kid might cozy up to the indie kid and put on her clothes if ripped jeans, Chuck Taylor shoes, and worn out leather jackets suddenly become stylish.

Martin is the popular kid borrowing the indie kid's leather jacket—or better, he took the indie kids, gave them a haircut, and washed their tattered jeans so they could sit at the popular table. He plucked "Maps" from the burgeoning musical periphery and molded it into "Since U Been Gone" for a broad audience.

But to understand the copy, we first have to know the original. What is the song trying to say? How does it say it? What needed updating? Answering these questions can reveal what makes one indie and the other pop.

"Maps" is a breakup song that reads like avant-garde poetry, creating an indie aesthetic through its economy of words. The entire song comprises only twenty-six words, its verses made up of monosyllabic pairings ("pack up/I'm straight"). There are few narrative details to clue us in to the song's meaning, and even the title, "Maps," is not explicated by the lyrics. The title is instead obscured: the single syllable word is drawn out in a long melisma that alternates between two notes drawn across two full bars of music ("Ma-a-a/a-a-a/a-a-a/a-a-aps"). Indie music blogs claim that "Maps" is in fact an acronym for "my Angus, please stay," referring to Karen O's boyfriend at the time, and it's also been suggested that the title may be a nautical reference tracing the geography of the relationship. None of this can be supported by the lyrics themselves. What we do know: the singer's lover is packing up to leave and she pleads with him to "wait" because no other lover could "love you like I love you." This is a classic breakup song.

Instead of providing detailed descriptions of her emotional state, Karen O conveys how she feels through the repetition of lyrical and musical material. The phrase "oh say say say" is repeated in the verse. Rather than expand or "say" much at all, Karen O moves on to another repeated word in the song. "Maps" is the title word of the song, and shares something in common with the "oh say" phrase. Both use a similar melodic motif that rocks between the pitches D and B.

This motif is established in the first words of the verse "pack up," and then recycled in both the repeated "say" and "maps" phrases. The stretched-out syllables repeat with hypnotic simplicity, pleading incessantly through short, repeated musical phrasing. Pulling the listener into the all-consuming waves of sadness, the song illustrates the aching pains of breakup through lyrical and musical repetition.

"Maps" is inherently anti-pop in both form and production. It sounds as if it was recorded in a single take in a garage. There are no frills or overdubs. The music video reinforces this message—the camera opens on a film set, and we see the scaffolding of background lighting in a small loft venue. The director announces "lights, camera, action," as if we are witnessing the original recording. The song then begins with an extended intro in which frail, arrhythmic notes on a guitar contrast with warlike, beating drums. This backdrop is open and raw, just like the singer. The song fills in during the chorus with bass and guitar, but where a standard chorus would be an energetic high point, the chorus of "Maps" is both musically and lyrically low. Karen O moves the melody on "they don't love you like I love you," to the lowest notes in the song, at the bottom of her range. Our expectations of traditional song form are broken, to emphasize the emotional lows of the breakup. The melodic descent also facilitates the move to the bridge, or in punk parlance, the breakdown (1:57). Right after the chorus, the voices cut out, and the instruments play the bridge section in fierce unison—twice. Pop listeners might be surprised by the guitars blasting out pent-up anger, as a bridge is typically more reserved, a moment for the song to catch its breath before a final chorus. But Yeah Yeah Yeahs is playing to a different audience. This anxious breakdown reaches out to those indie kids in their torn jeans who enjoy breaking conventions.

"Maps" is subversive and indirect, somber and affective in its subtleties and abnormalities. It is these qualities that make "Maps" an indie success—and these same indie tendencies are precisely what Martin refashions in his pop remake. He lifts all of the sonic qualities, raw emotions, and musical motifs, and

FIGURE 15.1 Three note motif of "Maps" (15.1a) reinterpreted in "Since U Been Gone" (15.1b).

superimposes them on a lyrical narrative, traditional song form, and high-fidelity pop production. "Since U Been Gone" does not hide its source material. Just like "Maps," the song opens with a solo guitar in the same key of G major. The first notes and rhythms of the lyrics even derive from the original. Clarkson's opening line "here's the thing" is adapted from the same three-note phrase that Karen O sings over "pack up" (Figure 15.1).

"Since" updates this material and polishes it into a pop format by giving the song a narrative arc. If indie music is intentionally obfuscated, pop needs to be approachable, accessible, if not in-your-face obvious. Listeners don't have to guess what "Since U Been Gone" is about—they're told directly in the title, which occurs as a catchy hook that repeats in every verse and chorus a total of twelve times. In "Maps," listeners have to make it through thirty seconds of distorted guitars and beating drums before they even get to hear the song's first lyric. "Since" gets straight to the point—the guitar intro lasts just three seconds before the vocals enter. "Maps" blows all its energy in the vigorous drum intro. "Since" uses a stark electronic drum kit to let the musical tension grow with the song's narrative.

Martin updates the spartan indie lyrics with a saccharine breakup story: a friendship turns into a relationship with commitment problems (verse), that builds into a breakup (pre-chorus), that explodes into an anthem celebrating singledom (chorus). There is nothing cryptic about the lyrics. "Maps" sustains its ambiguity through repetition and dwells on the painful breakup. "Since" brushes over the difficult part of the breakup and quickly moves on. In the chorus, the singer catches a breath for one beat, refocuses, and gets what she wants: to be single. Years of therapy are condensed into a three-minute pop song. If only it were so easy.

Just as the lyrics open up into a fuller story, so does the music. Instead of repeating the same melodic motif until the chorus, "Since U Been Gone" expands the three-note "Maps" theme right in the verse. The motif begins on the first line: "Here's the thing" is repeated once, and then is paired with an interpolated version of the chorus from "Maps." The descending chorus melody "They don't like you like I love you" becomes the second phrase of the verse for "Since": "It was cool, but it was all pretend." The ups and downs of the relationship unfold in the first stanza of music. This song is ready to move on as soon as we've walked in the door.

The melody isn't the only repurposed material. The same high-pitched guitar from the introduction to "Maps" is grafted onto "Since." But rather than use them as constant background material, "Since" employs the guitar line to build tension in the pre-chorus. Underneath, feedback from another distorted guitar gradually rises, building up to the moment we have all been waiting for: the chorus.

The chorus is the missing piece that transforms "Maps" into a Billboard-ready single. The chorus's sole task is to imprint its melodic hook and message into pop listeners' ears. Instead of subverting our expectations with a downer chorus in "Maps," "Since" delivers a soaring climax. The indie sensibility is discarded, and the chorus is straight glam rock. The terse sound of electronic percussion is overtaken by raucous live druming.

Clarkson exalts in the freedom of being single, belting notes into the high range of her voice where she can sing most freely and gloriously. Supporting her is a chorus of . . . herself. Stacks of Clarkson's vocals are doubled and harmonies are added to surround the stereo field. She's louder and bolder than she was in the verse, all the way back when the relationship took place. No past lover could possibly pierce her heart through this magnificent wall of self-confident sound. This vibrant vocal production seems to scream "I'm a pop song!" Tuned vocals and perfectly aligned backing tracks are a hallmark of contemporary pop production. At this point in the song, there is not one sonic fingerprint left over from the sullen "Maps."

If "Maps" is an indie hit because of how it subverts pop narrative and form, "Since" is a pop success because of how it inverts "Maps." The heartbreak that saturates "Maps" appears in just the first forty seconds of "Since." The high-pitched guitar, the drums, the melodic motifs, the brooding are all squeezed together to create a setup for the hook. Martin and friends establish this aesthetic in the verse and pre-chorus only to later transcend it in the chorus. "Maps" is like the long drawn-out and repeating opening to "Stairway to Heaven" (1971) and "Since" is the soaring guitar solo everyone is waiting for at the end.

But Martin isn't finished with "Maps"; the punk part of the song is yet to come. The Yeah Yeah Yeahs saved the peak energy in their song for the wordless breakdown. If there is any personal catharsis in "Maps," it comes through in the explosive guitar line of the bridge. The distress of heartbreak is exemplified by this churning instrumental section. But it only works as the high point in the song because the chorus was so subdued. Had Karen O written a Max Martin-esque chorus, there would have been no room for the high energy in the breakdown.

The musical interlude in "Since" (2:04) is a close copy of the "Maps" breakdown (1:57). Similar chugging guitars hit the same notes and rhythms, as beating toms push the music forward. But in "Since," this breakdown is transitory and doesn't function as the central high of the song. In standard pop format the bridge is submissive to the chorus, so to fit this material into "Since," the drums are tamed and the riff is played by a single guitar instead of three. Rather than give everything away at once, feedback from the guitar rises gradually and the drum toms take over. The bridge builds over eight bars to the point where it bursts right back into the meteoric chorus—the chorus that "Maps" is missing.

"Since U Been Gone" cannibalizes the hard edges from "Maps," using the same biting guitars and throbbing drums and repurposing the verse melody and breakdown. So what makes "Since" immediately recognizable as a pop song? The answer is in how "Maps" is transformed to become "Since." The pop version contains elements that define it as pop: the all-important hook, a transparent narrative, vocal production choices, rising melodic tension, and adherence to a verse-chorus structure in which each section performs its expected duty. Pop is recognizable not by the sound of any one part but by the way it assembles those discrete parts and smooths them out for mass appeal.

Pop's consumption of other genres doesn't apply just to indie rock. Pop is always a chameleon, changing its colors to the sound of the moment. The guitar-oriented rock of the '60s British Invasion band the Rolling Stones was appropriated from African American blues artist Muddy Waters—they even took their name from his song "Rollin' Stone" (1950), as did the magazine. Madonna's "Vogue" (1990) drew from house music, which for a decade had defined the sound of underground queer spaces. Dr. Dre reimagined funk from the '70s to create the West Coast hip hop sound of the '90s. Reinventing his sound for the 2010s, Martin tamed the explosiveness of EDM to compose Ariana Grande's "No Tears Left to Cry" (2018). Each decade of pop comprises dozens of different sounds drawn from sub-genres of music. Deft songwriters like Martin braid new sounds into a familiar pop format that can break into the mainstream. While sounds may change by the season, song structures and production techniques are much slower to evolve. These standardized forms help keep popular music consistent and recognizable over many decades (see Chapter 4 on song form).

Just like adolescent fashion, genres wax and wane in popularity, yet the aim of mainstream music stays the same: to appeal to large audiences. To stay current, pop trendsetters absorb sounds from outside of the mainstream, often originating with marginalized groups, and appropriate these sounds into a pop format. Even though pop music undergoes annual makeovers, listeners can identify the musical stitching, which is consistent across decades. And though pop music may seem like a young person's pursuit, musical manufacturers like Martin can sustain a career by draping their songs in the newest sounds, in an ever-expanding and always stylish wardrobe.

I Like Everything . . . Except Country and Hip Hop

Musical Identity: Jay Z and Kanye West ft. Frank Ocean | Toby Keith—"Made in America"

In the summer of 2011 two songs titled "Made in America" were born. Despite sharing a name and release date, the tracks could not have been more different. One "Made in America" came from outspoken country music star Toby Keith, the larger-than-life patriot who in his post-9/11 hit "Courtesy of the Red, White, and Blue" (2001) threatened the whole world: "We'll put a boot in your ass/It's the American way." The other "Made in America" came from Jay Z and Kanye West, featuring Frank Ocean, a trio approaching mythical status in the world of hip hop for their pioneering flows, beats, and vocals. The stars-and-stripes-crossed destiny of these two tracks presents an intriguing opportunity to analyze both versions of "Made in America" and explore the

"Made In America" performed by Toby Keith, written by Keith, Bobby Pinson, Scott Reeves, Show Dog-Universal Music, 2011.

"Made In America" performed by Jay Z and Kanye West featuring Frank Ocean, written by West, Shawn Carter, Christopher Breaux, Mike Dean, Joseph Roach, Roc-A-Fella/Def Jam/Roc Nation, 2011).

relationship between sound and style. Of all popular genres, country music and hip hop appear the most diametrically opposed, separated by race, geography, and politics, by the Billboard charts and the radio dial. Comparing two disparate songs with the same title allows us to ask a question borrowed from musicologist Kofi Agawu—not "What do these songs mean?" but rather "*How* do these songs mean?" The answer has a lot to do with timbre. Hear a banjo or a vocal "twang" and you immediately think country; hear programmed drums and rapped lyrics and your mind goes to hip hop. The associations are clear, but why? To find the answer, we need to take key timbral elements of each style—banjo and twang, drums and rap—and trace their paths to musical meaning.

First, we need to hear how each describes what it is to be "made in America." Toby Keith's song focuses on the narrator's father, a working-class family man "born in the heartland" with "dirty hands and a clean soul." The Nashville songwriting team behind Keith's hit deliver more background in the chorus: "He's got the red, white, and blue flying high on the farm/Semper Fi tattooed on his left arm." With one couplet, Keith communicates values of rural life, patriotism, and military service—Semper Fidelis, or "always faithful," is the Latin motto of the United States Marine Corps. The lyrics of this "Made in America" often verge on cliché, but two lines are worth a close listen: "It breaks his heart seeing foreign cars/filled with fuel that isn't ours." Chevys and Fords are almost compulsory in a country song—but the reference here to cars manufactured abroad reflects the rapid and recent decline of the US auto industry, and the pain of lost blue-collar jobs rings true. There's a poignant nostalgia in the track's yearning for a golden age.

Jay Z, Kanye West, and Frank Ocean also confront the past in their "Made in America," but for them it is a site of struggle rather than of lost glory. Ocean's sung introduction casts civil rights leaders of the 1960s as holy figures, Martin Luther King Jr. and Coretta Scott King becoming "Sweet King Martin" and "Sweet Queen Coretta." His invocation ends with a revised version of the song's title: instead of "made in America," he sings "We made it in America." The change is small but significant, signaling a vision of a nation that presents more obstacles than opportunities. Jay Z delves further into the idea in his verse, joking that "Our apple pie was supplied by Arm and Hammer." It's a clever line, implying both Jay Z's fractured experience of the "American dream" of baseball and apple pie as well as his involvement in the illegal drug trade, since baking soda can be used to cut cocaine. Jay's references elsewhere to the "streets" places listeners far from the rural heartland, but there's overlap with Keith's world—values of community, the working class, religion. There's patriotism too, of a jaded sort. Jay calls out the country's structural injustice and imagines a better nation: "I pledge allegiance to all the scramblers/This is my Star Spangled Banner."

The timbres of each song reinforce its respective values and cultural contexts. The deep twang in Keith's delivery is a crucial element of his working-class vocals. Defined by country music scholar Jocelyn Neal as the product of a "tight throat" and a "nasal whine," the twang immediately conjures the South. It's a tough tone, connected to the sense of "longing and loss" that defined the region's deep and defiant Calvinist religious tradition. The twang is also closely related to Keith's southern accent, such an essential sound in the modern country palette that even country musicians like Keith Urban, who hails from Australia, adopt it in their music.

The banjo that enters the song at :11 is another twangy instrument, one intimately associated with country music. But its twang has a different source. The ancestors of the modern banjo were African stringed instruments such as the *ngoni*, made by stretching a membrane over a hollowed-out gourd, brought to the South via the transatlantic slave trade. Later crafted out of metal brackets and wooden hoops, the banjo continued to play a role in African American culture in minstrelsy of the 1800s, then urban jazz and ragtime of the early 1900s, before dropping out of fashion in the 1930s in favor of the guitar. Not until the twenty-first century was the black banjo reintroduced by artists like Rhiannon Giddens and Tony Thomas, recovering and reclaiming the tradition of early African American music. Before this, country music adopted the instrument, and its African origins and associations fell away for almost a century. The banjo became a staple in bluegrass music, popularized by the three-finger picking of Earl Scruggs. By the time the 1972 film *Deliverance* featured a young boy ominously plucking "Duelin' Banjos" on a backwoods porch, the banjo had long crossed over into its modern associations with white, southern, rural music. In the process, the meaning of its twang was reinscribed. The banjo's connection to West African musical practice was lost, and a new connection with vocal twang was established.

The timbres throughout Jay Z and Kanye West's "Made in America" are no less significant, referring back to the history and diversity of black music in the US. Jay Z's percussive flow creates a sonic analog to his lyrical message of individual and collective struggle. His rough vocal timbre is informed by a rap style established in the 1990s as hip hop became more overtly political, a kind of "scream for the unheard." In addition, Jay Z adds a particular effect into the rhythmic pattern of his lyrics—non-verbal grunts interjected between words and phrases: "[unh] I pledge allegiance [unh] to all the scramblers [unh]." These sounds are part of his flow, what the critic Jelani Cobb defines as "an individual time signature, the rapper's own idiosyncratic approach to the use of time." A heavy dose of grunts in his flow on "Made in America" connects Jay Z to a long lineage of singers who have employed vocal utterances: Louis Armstrong, Aretha Franklin,

Prince. These husky interjections give the lyrics a propulsive forward momentum as they also communicate a sense of history, of decades of effort, striving, and scrambling by black musicians.

The beat, produced by Sak Pase and Mike Dean, reinforces Jay Z's gravelly vocal timbre. Electronic instruments saturate the song, a combination of synthesized pads, drums, and piano. There is one other distinctive texture in the beat—a harsh, high-pitched electronic burst that occurs on every second and fourth pulse, sounding like the repetitive "beep" of a delivery truck in reverse. That beep is actually is the "cowbell" sound from the Roland TR-808 drum machine, processed, deteriorated, and stretched out. It has a rough, tinny sound that indexes the history of hip hop, a genre that depended on repurposing affordable technology like the 808. The TR-808 was developed in 1980 by Japan's Roland Corporation as a device for making demo recordings. In other words, not a star instrument, just an easy way to create a groove and play it over into a tape recorder. Marvin Gaye featured an unfiltered 808 in "Sexual Healing" (1982), but most musicians didn't appreciate the 808's idiosyncratic drum tones, and by 1983 the instrument was discontinued. Hip hop producers picked up discarded 808s at pawn shops and began to experiment with the used piece of hardware. Jermaine Dupri thickened the sound of the drum machine when he used it in Mariah Carey's 1995 hit "Always Be My Baby." "Get Low" by Lil Jon and the Eastside Boyz (2002) deepened the 808 bass drum further, to almost body-buzzing dimensions. Gucci Mane's "I Get the Bag" featuring Migos (2017) shows the final important tweak from the original demo machine to its current role: adding pitch to the bass drum so it becomes its own subterranean melody. By the time Sak Pase and Mike Dean used it on "Made in America," generations of producers had made the 808 so synonymous with hip hop that its name acts as shorthand for any deep bass drum in a track. As Big Boi raps on "I Like the Way

You Move" (2003), "But I know y'all wanted that 808/Can you feel that B-A-S-S bass?"

While the banjo and 808 are now core parts of the sound of country and hip hop, each instrument was repurposed from its original function. Taking apart the timbres in either "Made in America" shows us that the meanings of sounds aren't fixed. They are unstable and constantly subject to revision. In turn, genres are more porous than they might seem. Some aspects like twang and flow connect back to the earliest roots of the style, whereas others like the banjo and the 808 have migrated from different styles and cultures entirely. Each song is full of rogue timbres from cultural exchange. The piano that enters at :34 in Jay Z and company's "Made in America" links to a lineage of rock and roll keyboard playing dating back to Little Richard. The electric guitar that opens Keith's "Made in America" also comes from rock, its unique tone the product of timbral manipulation through delay, reverb, and distortion, an effect more reminiscent of the arena rock of U2 than of a country icon like Hank Williams. The electric organ that slides into Keith's song in the second verse (1:22) can be traced to African American gospel tradition, and so can the prayerful vocals of Frank Ocean.

Given that hip hop and country are both full of different timbres, it is worth considering why such strong genre associations persist around certain sounds in country and hip hop. For historian Karl Hagstrom Miller the answer is in part that record companies and music promoters during the 1920s and 1930s deliberately segregated the diverse sounds of southern music into narrow racial categories that would target specific audiences and maximize profits. The Billboard charts followed suit, dividing southern music into two racially distinct categories: "Hillbilly Hits" and the "Harlem Hit Parade." The names have since changed to "Country Singles" and "Hot R&B," but the division persists. Even as the music industry segregated sound, musicians resisted such reductive binaries. In 1930, the most popular "hillbilly" singer of the time, Jimmie Rodgers, cut "Blue Yodel #9" in collaboration with jazz trumpeter Louis Armstrong and pianist Lil Hardin Armstrong. In the 1950s and 1960s soul singer Solomon Burke released a string of country hits, including "Just Out of Reach" (1962), which was later covered by country artist Patsy Cline. The same year, Ray Charles recorded the album *Modern Sounds in Country and Western Music*, and in 1992 Whitney Houston's hit "I Will Always Love You" remade Dolly Parton's 1974 country original. In 2012, country duo Florida Georgia Line collaborated with the rapper Nelly for the remix of their song "Cruise," which became the best-selling digital country single until that point. In 2019, Lil Nas X and Billy Ray Cyrus merged trap and country in the hit song "Old Town Road." In short, music has always trespassed the borders of genre. Burke's country songs were so popular with white audiences that he claimed he was once booked to play a Klu Klux Klan rally in Mississippi, its organizers having not realized that Burke was, in fact, black. Burke's tale may be apocryphal, but it exposes how our perceptions of musical difference are less motivated by the ear than by the eye.

Genre isn't just a matter of musical taste gravitating toward certain timbres; genre is a matter of identity. As scholar Nadine Hubbs writes, when people say "I like every type of music . . . except country," they're not just dismissing the style, but they're intentionally separating themselves from people who listen to country (or rather, the people they imagine listen to country). There are high stakes at play in our construction of timbral meaning. Whether we hear a banjo as belonging to country or West African music isn't simply a matter of musical preference but of which parts of U.S. history we want to highlight or identify with. The borders of genres as constructed through timbral meaning gets at the heart of American music—a national music contending with competing narratives of cultural exceptionalism and imperialism. At the same time, genres aren't stable. They shift over time as different timbres pass through them. The better we understand how sound creates meaning and where that meaning comes from, the better we can understand how genre does its work. Only then we can really hear what it means to be made in America.

Conclusion

The Past, Present, and Future of Silly Little Love Songs

Paul McCartney—"Get Enough"

On New Year's Day 2019, the most successful songwriter of all time released his most unusual single in decades, "Get Enough." For Sir Paul McCartney, like many, another trip around the sun is a time for reflection. The song starts sparsely, just McCartney and a solo piano. The piano moves between chords while McCartney wistfully remembers strolling by the shore with a long-lost lover. In a low baritone, McCartney sings of two lovers watching the moon cast its rippling light onto the ocean's horizon. As the moon sets westward, the septuagenarian songwriter tries to hold onto this fleeting moment, interrupting the flashback—"Do you remember?"—a line he wistfully repeats three more times throughout the song. Yet the way he sings the lyric belies his own request to go back in time. His vocal harmonies, coated in an Auto-Tune effect, land McCartney thoroughly in the present, moving ahead, modern timbres, technology and all. McCartney has penned 736 songs (192 as Lennon-McCartney), many of them timeless classics, and released 36 albums since the Beatles

"Get Enough" performed by Paul McCartney, written by McCartney, Ryan Tedder, Zach Skelton, Capitol Records, 2019.

broke up, an average of one every year and a half. He has made musical forays into disco, opera, classical, and techno—but he always returns to the silly little love songs of pop. "Get Enough" may not be a Top 40 hit, but it stands as an allegory for the whole of popular music, which circles back to the past as it marches into the future.

It may seem scandalous to Auto-Tune a knight's hallowed voice, but this isn't the first time McCartney has dabbled in the effect. Collaborating with Kanye West on "Only One" (2014), McCartney's background vocal undergoes a robotic transformation beyond the point of recognition. Conversely, the Auto-Tune on "Get Enough" seems to humanize the legendary songwriter by processing his vocal just like any other singer on the 2019 Billboard charts. The unexpected effect also highlights the "do you remember?" lyric, placing the song in a liminal space between the singer's past and the song's present. But conspicuous Auto-Tune is only the first of many contemporary references. By enlisting co-writers Ryan Tedder and Zach Skelton (whose combined credits include Beyoncé, Demi Lovato, Logic, Selena Gomez, and Shawn Mendes among many others), McCartney signals that he is ready, willing, and able to adapt to the changing sounds of pop.

As the song builds, it adds in more modern textures. In the chorus, McCartney covers the naked piano with warm synth pads and deep bass tones. McCartney ornaments the chorus with audible grunts, a seeming nod to Jay Z's staple rhythmic utterance heard in Chapter 16: "unh" (:51). The hook repeats "get enough, get enough, get enough" followed by a long "ooooooh" manipulated into a Skrillex-esque synthesizer. Present-day production techniques put this hybrid high-pitched synth-voice in counterpoint with McCartney's main vocal (1:40). Even the brevity of the song (2:57) and its streaming-only release depart from McCartney's album-oriented musical suites on *Abbey Road*

(1969) and *Band on the Run* (1973). Lifelong McCartney acolytes might wonder why he is deviating so far from their favorite music of yesteryear, especially in a song that reminisces about the past.

The contemporary production is a masterful foil for the song's next section. The second chorus builds with an ascending bass line, pointing optimistically upward. Then, the song crescendos with a Ringo Starr-style drum fill that leads into a bold upward modulation to the key of A-flat major (1:58). This new key transports us into the musical past. Multiple acoustic guitars strum along to dreamy drums, with a chorus of McCartneys harmonizing joyously—"ahh!"—this time with no audible vocal manipulation, just a carefree and natural sound that harkens back to the earliest Beatles recordings. Then, deep in the mix, a barely audible, mysterious spoken voice recites the lyric: "I think maybe I should, go back to nature, traditional." The classic timbres in the bridge are the "traditional" sounds that McCartney fans expect. These timbres serve as a memory palace for McCartney's long-lost love. In the midst of this nostalgic recollection, the bridge chords take a disorienting minor turn, much like the outro of the Beatles' "A Day in the Life" (1967).

Suddenly, the song shifts back to the original key of F major, the guitars and drums cut out, and the piano chords from the introduction return. It's as if the present has caught back up to McCartney. The old sounds fade away, the contemporary production comes back, and McCartney intones "get enough" six times, his voice cracking. On the final refrain, the past merges with the present: over his raw voice the Auto-Tune harmonies recur: "I can't get enough, enough of you." Who is this, "you," anyway? By song's end, it feels like McCartney's object of affection is pop itself, the sound he "can't get enough" of. As the piano fades into the distance, we, Sir Paul, and all of pop music, keep moving ahead.

Acknowledgments

Since its inception, *Switched On Pop* has been a collaborative process between two friends and thousands of listeners around the world. That conversation has made us better listeners, smarter thinkers, and pushed the show in new directions. Our gratitude to all who have tuned in cannot be overstated. Thanks to Sarah Lazin for guiding us every step of the way and shepherding this book into existence, Julia Conrad for coming up with the idea of a *Switched On* book and whipping our proposal into shape, and Margaret Shultz and Catherine Strong for all their assistance. Huge thanks to Suzanne Ryan of Oxford University Press, the most joyous, knowledgeable, and supportive editor anyone could ever ask for; and to Victoria Dixon for her tireless work on this project. We wish to thank all of the friends, family, readers, teachers, and guests who have helped support and build this show and book: Yukiko Adachi, Jocelyn Adams, Udi Assaf, Raisa Aziz, Robin Bell, Alex Blau, Clare Bokulich, Rob Bonstein, Breakmaster Cylinder, Mollie Chen, Arlene Cole, Kwami Coleman, Will Daly, the Davis family, Patrick Cook Deegan, Gina Delvac, Maciek Dolata, Chris Duffy, Samantha Feinberg, Lucas Foglia, Tyler Gage, Sam Goldman, Iris Gottlieb, Karen, John, Elle, Haydn, and Frances Graham; James T. Green, Steve Hall, Chip Harding, Henry A., Henry B., and Mary Harding, Peggy Harding, Dave

Harrington, Luke Harris, Paul Heck, Quinn Heraty, Hrishikesh Hirway, Jessica Holmes, Linda Holmes, William Hutson, Gideon Irving, Jake Izenberg, Robin James, Tom Kalb, Susan Kamenar, Alex Kapelman, Ezra Klein, Zoe Komarin, Dan Kopf, Mark Kross, Nishat Kurwa, Bill Lancz, Evan Lang, Nathaniel and Stephanie Lepp, Andrew Lim, Matt Lindeboom, Jeremy Lloyd, Michael Maffattone, Nathaniel and Sunisa Manning, Andrew Marantz, Allyson Marino, Brandon McFarland, Sarah Megan, Hannah Mintz, Chris Molanphy, Zach Tenorio Miller, Charlie Moore, Drew Nobile, Abby Olitzky, Calla Ostrander, Morgan Page, Asaf Peres, Chris Pergolizzi, Katie Richmond, Benjamin Riskin, Kevin Roose, Erica Rosen, Micah Salkind, Bill Sellanga, Stef Simons, Leo, Randi, and Bob Sloan, Jimmy Smagula, Jonathan Snipes, Moses Soyoola, Ramesh Srinivasan, Trevor Stutz, Sarah Terry, Kathy Tu, Lisa Cooper Vest, Cher Vincent, Sebo Walker, Jillian Weinberger, Margaret H. Willison, Steve Wilson, Lucas Wittman, Ali Wollner, Olivia Wood, Helen Zaltzman. Special thanks to Bess Kalb and Whitney Rose Graham, who are the reason that silly little love songs exist. To all the listeners wanting a book about pop: we hope it was worth the wait.

Notes

Introduction

3   *In a 2014 article for Slate, the musician Owen Pallett*: Owen Pallett, "Skin Tight Jeans and Syncopation," *Slate*, March 25, 2014.

6–7   *songwriter Emily Warren told us*: "The Side Effects of Pop Music (with Emily Warren)," *Switched On Pop* (podcast), September 18, 2018.

6–7   *Sia replied*: Hillel Aron, "How Sia Saved Herself," *Rolling Stone*, August 24, 2018.

7–8   *As the cultural theorist Stuart Hall has noted*: Stuart Hall, "Notes on Deconstructing 'the Popular,'" in *People's History and Socialist Theory*, ed. R. Samuel (London: Routledge, 1981).

Chapter 1

11   *Humans have upper and lower limits to the tempo that we can process*: D. Moelants, "Preferred Tempo Reconsidered," in *Proceedings of the 7th International Conference on Music Perception and Cognition*, ed. C. Stevens, D. Burnham, G. McPherson, E. Schubert, and J. Renwick (Sydney, Adelaide: Casual Productions, 2002), 580–583.

11   *they also like to walk at about 120 steps per minute*: Hamish G. MacDougall and Steven T. Moore, "Marching to the Beat of the Same Drummer: The Spontaneous Tempo of Human

Locomotion," *Journal of Applied Physiology* 99, no. 3 (2005), 1164–1173.

14   *In 1900, one music magazine writing about ragtime*: Edward Berlin, *Ragtime: A Musical and Cultural History* (Berkeley: University of California Press, 1984), 44.

14   *The same language of race and pathology*: Nicolas Slonimsky, *Lexicon of Musical Invective* (New York: W.W. Norton, 2000), 25; Tricia Rose, *The Hip Hop Wars* (New York: Basic Books, 2008), 36.

14–15   *Jose Feliciano sang the "Star-Spangled Banner" as a folk song*: Victor Mather, "A Polarizing Anthem Performance—by Jose Feliciano in 1968," *New York Times*, October 6, 2017, https://www.nytimes.com/2017/10/06/sports/baseball/national-anthem.html, accessed February 8, 2019.

14–15   *Houston's iconic rendition of the anthem*: Cinque Henderson, "Anthem of Freedom: How Whitney Houston Remade 'The Star-Spangled Banner,'" *New Yorker* (online), January 27, 2016, https://www.newyorker.com/culture/cultural-comment/anthem-of-freedom-how-whitney-houston-remade-the-star-spangled-banner, accessed February 8, 2019.

17   *Benjamin revealed a surprising fact*: Ali Shaheed Muhammad and Frannie Kelley, "Andre 3000: 'You Can Do Anything from Atlanta,'" *NPR Microphone Check Archive*, September 26, 2014, https://www.npr.org/sections/microphonecheck/2014/09/26/351559126/andre-3000-you-can-do-anything-from-atlanta, accessed February 6, 2019.

18–19   *when Benjamin released "Hey Ya!" he was nervous*: Soren Baker, "Andrew 3000 on Releasing 'Hey Ya!': 'I Was Terrified,'" *HipHopDX*, October 2, 2014, https://hiphopdx.com/news/id.30903/title.andre-3000-on-releasing-hey-ya-i-was-terrified#signup, accessed February 7, 2019.

18–19   *He recorded every instrument*: Will Welch, "Earth to André 3000: The OutKast Icon Talks Life after 'Hey Ya!'" *GQ*, October 30, 2017.

19–20   *one of the ten most-played songs at weddings*: Ben Zauzmer, "These Are the Most Popular Wedding Songs in America—and the Ones Your State Loves," *Washington Post*, September

20, 2017, https://www.washingtonpost.com/news/soloish/wp/2017/09/20/these-are-the-most-popular-wedding-songs-in-america-and-the-ones-your-state-loves/?utm_term=.7bdc15f4a275, accessed February 8, 2019.

Chapter 2

25   *Igor Stravinsky*: Igor Stravinsky, *Poetics of Music in the Form of Six Lessons* (Cambridge, MA: Harvard University Press, 1970), 64.

25   *Jacob Collier*: Jacob Collier, Twitter, March 29, 2018.

27   *Taylor Swift, who as a child*: Vanessa Grigoriadis, "The Very Pink, Very Perfect Life of Taylor Swift," *Rolling Stone*, March 5, 2009.

28   *"more like Morse code than music"*: Katherine Bergeron, *Voice Lessons: French Melodies in the Belle Époque* (New York: Oxford University Press, 2010), 312.

28   *Swift herself uses this technique*: Mark Savage, "Why Does Taylor Swift Write So Many One-Note Melodies," *BBC News*, November 8, 2017.

28–29 *Paul Simon*: Walter Everett, "Swallowed by a Song: Paul Simon's Crisis of Chromaticism," in *Understanding Rock: Essays in Musical Analysis*, ed. John Covach and Graeme Boone (New York: Oxford University Press, 1997).

32–33 *Josquin used this melodic combination a total of 704 times*: We know this exact number thanks to the efforts of the Josquin Research Project (josquin.stanford.edu), a team led by musicologists Jesse Rodin, Craig Sapp, and Clare Bokulich that has digitized and made searchable every note ever put down by the great composer of Catholic liturgical music. One can only imagine what will be learned about other artists' melodic proclivities once scholars create the Taylor Swift Research Project (and the Beyoncé Research Project, the Michael Jackson Research Project, etc.). Until then, less scientific methodology will have to suffice—namely, listening closely to a ton of music.

33   *"funny and knowing"*: Jon Caramanica, "A Farewell to Twang," *New York Times*, October 23, 2014.

33–34   *Ellie Goulding*: Louise Gannon, "All I Wanted to Be Was Strong" *Elle UK*, July 2015, 116.

33–34   *Kristin Lieb*: Kristin Lieb, *Gender, Branding, and the Modern Music Industry* (New York: Routledge, 2015), 81.

34–35   *As Swift explained*: Randy Lewis, "She's Writing Her Future," *Los Angeles Times*, October 26, 2008.

34–35   *Prokofiev's producer*: Simon Morrison, *The People's Artist: Prokofiev's Soviet Years* (New York: Oxford University Press, 2010), 37.

Chapter 3

40   *One of Rameau's biographers*: Thomas Christensen, *Rameau and Musical Thought in the Enlightenment* (Cambridge: Cambridge University Press, 2004), 132.

44   *"Blues in the verse and gospel in the chorus."*: Jack Antonoff, "Jack Antonoff on How to Write a Perfect Pop Song," *New York Magazine*, June 26, 2017.

45   *forty separate vocal takes*: Paul Tingen, "Jeff Bhasker on Mixing 'We Are Young,'" *Sound on Sound*, October, 2012, https://www.soundonsound.com/people/jeff-bhasker-mixing-we-are-young.

Chapter 4

49–50   *Calvin Harris DJ'ed a set in Ibiza in 2015*: Calvin Harris, "Radio 1 DJ Set," YouTube video, 22:48, July 31, 2015, https://www.youtube.com/watch?v=QylU_gVpJbo.

50–51   *music theorist Asaf Peres*: Asaf Peres, "Everything You Need to Know about the Postchorus," *Top 40 Theory*, July 31, 2018, https://www.top40theory.com/blog/everything-you-need-to-know-about-the-postchorus, accessed July 8, 2018.

Chapter 5

55   *YouTube comments*: PopCrush, "Sia's Best Live Vocals," YouTube video, 5:11, February 4, 2016, https://www.youtube.com/watch?v=bltLjnMw9bA.

56   *Sia decided*: Sam Sanders, "A Reluctant Star, Sia Deals with Fame on Her Own Terms," *NPR Morning Edition*, July 8, 2014.

56   *two massive hit songs that she wrote and recorded as demos*: Phil Gallo, "Sia: The Billboard Cover Story," *Billboard*, October 25, 2013.

56   *her ambition to remain anonymous ends up being what makes her recognizable*: Kai Arne Hansen, "Holding On for Dear Life: Gender, Celebrity Status and Vulnerability-on-Display in Sia's 'Chandelier,'" in *The Routledge Research Companion to Popular Music and Gender*, ed. Stan Hawkins (London: Routledge, 2017).

56   *focus on her musical technique*: Robin James, "These Are Sia's Breaks: On Vocal Technique and Queering Feminine Resistance," *It's Her Factory* (blog), April 1, 2016, https://www.its-her-factory.com/2016/04/these-are-sias-breaks-on-vocal-technique-queering-feminine-resilience/.

56–57   *height, length, depth*: Robert Fink, Melinda Latour, and Zachary Wallmark, "Introduction," in *The Relentless Pursuit of Tone* (New York: Oxford University Press, 2018), 9.

56–57   *motor resonance is involved in the processing of timbre*: Zachary Wallmark et al., "Embodied Listening and Timbre: Perceptual, Acoustical, and Neural Correlates," *Music Perception* 35, no. 3 (2018), 357.

57–58   *felt more than heard*: David Font-Navarette, "Bass 101: Miami, Rio, and the Global Music South," *Journal of Popular Music Studies* 27, no. 4 (2015), 490.

57–58   *sensing sound is not limited to vibration*: Jessica Holmes, "Expert Hearing beyond the Limits of Hearing: Music and Deafness," *Journal of the American Musicological Society* 70, no. 1 (2017), 189.

58–59   *stretching the output of the voice to its limits*: Robin James, "These Are Sia's Breaks," *It's Her Factory* (blog), April 1, 2016, https://www.its-her-factory.com/2016/04/these-are-sias-breaks-on-vocal-technique-queering-feminine-resilience/.

58–59   *"glottal flip"*: Donna Soto-Morettini, *Popular Singing and Style*, 2nd ed. (London: Bloomsbury, 2014), 87.

59   *the manner of a female goat*: James Stark, *Bel Canto: A History of Vocal Pedagogy* (Toronto: University of Toronto Press, 2003), 130.

59–60   *the reception of Dave Grohl and Alanis Morissette*: Aimee Cliff, "How Sia's Polarizing Vocals Have Invaded the Mainstream," *Fader*, January 21, 2016.

59–60   *growing space for women to be ugly, rough, and weird*: Sasha Geffen, "Radical Strain," *New Inquiry*, September 8, 2014.

60   "*fake patois*": Osvaldo Oyola "Everyone I Listen To, Fake Patois . . ." *Sounding Out!*, April 9, 2012 https://soundstudiesblog.com/2012/04/09/everyone-i-listen-to-fake-patois/.

60   *Sia's use of a Caribbean accent*: Nina Sun Eidsheim, "Marian Anderson and 'Sonic Blackness' in American Opera," *American Quarterly* 63, no. 3 (2011), 665.

60–61   *the Southern Ewe have as many as seventeen names for different drum strokes*:Kofi Agawu, *The African Imagination in Music* (New York: Oxford, 2016), 94.

61–62   *expensive sounds*:Taige Jensen, Graham Roberts, Alicia Desantis, and Yuliya Parshina-Kottas, "Bieber, Diplo and Skrillex Make a Hit," *New York Times* video, 8:03, August, 25, 2015, https://www.nytimes.com/video/arts/music/100000003872410/bieber-diplo-and-skrillex-make-a-hit.html.

61–62   *pricey, space-age tools*: Paul Tingen, "Trevor Muzzy: Recording Nicki Minaj's 'Starships,'" *Sound on Sound*, August, 2012, https://www.soundonsound.com/people/trevor-muzzy-recording-nicki-minajs-starships, accessed January 29, 2018.

Chapter 7

70   *We need more songs, man*: Chris Heath, "Quincy Jones Has a Story about That," *GQ*, January 29, 2018.

71–72   *Musicologist Charlie Kronengold*: Charles Kronengold, "Accidents, Hooks and Theory," *Popular Music* 24, no. 3 (2005), 386.

73   *I am not going to sing a grammatically incorrect lyric*: Nolan Feeney, "Ariana Grande Is Fully Aware That the Lyrics of

'Break Free' Make No Sense," *Time*, August 7, 2014, http://time.com/3088143/ariana-grande-break-free-lyrics/, accessed December 17, 2018.

73–74   *Martin's awkward lyrics*: John Seabrook, *The Song Machine* (New York: W.W. Norton, 2015).

76–77   *An augmented chord appears in Zedd's song "Stay"*: Asaf Peres, @Top40Theory, Twitter Post, September 30, 2018, 12:32 P.M. https://twitter.com/Top40Theory/status/1046482924567171073.

76–77   *The Beatles used it as a favorite device*: Walter Everett, *The Beatles as Musicians: Revolver through the Anthology* (New York: Oxford University Press, 1999), 291.

78   *Beethoven's Fifth Symphony as an example of an effective hook*: Jim Peterik, Dave Austin, and Cathy Lynn, *Songwriting for Dummies*, 2nd ed. (Hoboken, NJ: Wiley, 2010), 77.

78   *Those four notes*: Matthew Guerrieri, *The First Four Notes: Beethoven's Fifth and the Human Imagination* (New York: Vintage, 2014).

Chapter 8

79–80   *listeners today have even lazier ears*: Stephen Sondheim, *Finishing the Hat: Collected Lyrics (1954–1981) with Attendant Comments, Principles, Heresies, Grudges, Whines and Anecdotes* (New York: Knopf, 2010), xxvi.

79–80   *In hip hop, too, the use of perfect rhymes has dropped*: Hussein Hirjee and Daniel G. Brown, "Using Automated Rhyme Detection to Characterize Rhyming Style in Rap Music," *Empirical Musicology Review* 5, no. 4 (2010), 121–145.

79–80   *GZA of the Wu-Tang Clan*: GZA, "The Lost Art of Lyricism," *Cuepoint*, May 27, 2015.

79–80   *Sondheim and GZA have earned license to criticize*: Stephen Sondheim, "Night Waltz 1—The Sun Won't Set" (1979), from *A Little Night Music*; Raekwon Feat, Ghostface Killah, Inspectah Deck, and GZA, "Guillotine (Swordz)" (1995).

79–80   *And criticize, perhaps, they should*: The Black Eyed Peas, "My Humps" (2005); Robin Thicke, "Blurred Lines" (2013); Clean Bandit featuring Demi Lovato, "Solo" (2018).

80   *"catchy nursery rhymes"*: Insanul Ahmed, "Drake, 'Started from the Bottom'—The 50 Best Songs of 2013," *Complex*, December 2, 2013.

80   *streaming services pay royalties out per song*: Aisha Hassan and Dan Kopf, "The Reason Why Your Favorite Pop Songs Are Getting Shorter," *Quartz*, October 27, 2018, https://qz.com/quartzy/1438412/the-reason-why-your-favorite-pop-songs-are-getting-shorter/, accessed January 15, 2019.

80–81   *W. H. Auden*: W. H. Auden, *The Dyer's Hand and Other Essays* (New York: Vintage, 1989), 380.

82   *"After the Ball,"*: Philip Furia, *Poets of Tin Pan Alley: A History of America's Great Lyricists* (New York: Oxford University Press, 1992), 23.

82   *first pop hit ever*: David Suisman, *Selling Sounds: The Commercial Revolution in American Music* (Cambridge, MA: Harvard University Press, 2009), 27–32.

84   *Adele does this to moving effect*: "Hotline Hello," *Switched On Pop* (podcast), November 4, 2014.

84   *"Sometimes the truth don't rhyme."*: Thanks to Mike Posner for pointing out this lyric from 2013's "Acid Rain" when he was a guest on *Switched On Pop*. "Entering Beard Phase (with Mike Posner)," *Switched On Pop*, November 28, 2018.

84–85   *Singing rappers*: Simon Reynolds, "How Auto-Tune Revolutionized the Sound of Popular Music," *Pitchfork*, September 17, 2018, https://pitchfork.com/features/article/how-auto-tune-revolutionized-the-sound-of-popular-music/, accessed January 3, 2019.

85   *Neurologist Oliver Sacks*: Oliver Sacks, *Musicophilia: Tales of Music and the Brain* (New York: Knopf, 2007), 258.

Chapter 9

87   *"subjective time dilation,"*: Virginie van Wassenhove et al., "Psychological and Neural Mechanisms of Subjective Time Dilation," *Frontiers in Neuroscience*, April 26, 2011.

87–88   *Jonathan Berger*: Jonathan Berger, "How Music Hijacks Our Perception of Time," *Nautilus*, January 23, 2014.

89 *a study on music cognition*: Maria A. G. Witek et al., "Syncopation, Body-Movement, and Pleasure in Groove Music," *PLOS ONE*, April 16, 2014.

89–90 *lyrical trope used by blues and country singers*: See Charlie Poole, "If the River Was Whiskey" (1930); Muddy Waters, "Rollin' and Tumblin'" (1950); Taj Mahal, "Diving Duck Blues" (1968).

92 *Derek "MixedByAli" Ali*: Insanul Ahmed, "How to Make It in America: TDE's MixedByAli on Becoming an Audio Engineer," *Complex*, May 2, 2014.

92–93 *Migos rap the three syllables*: Estelle Caldwell, "Earworm: How Triplets Took Over Hip Hop," *Vox* video, 9:42, September 18, 2017, https://www.vox.com/2017/9/18/16328330/migos-triplet-flow-rap/.

93 *hi-hats in the chorus*: Justin Burton, *Posthuman Rap* (New York: Oxford University Press, 2017), 86.

93–94 *the origin point of trap hi-hats*: Shawn Setaro, "How Trap Music Came to Rule the World," *Complex*, February 14, 2018.

94 *For Longstreth, the expressive potential of trap hats proved revelatory*: "How Dirty Projectors Make You Feel Energy," *Switched On Pop*, podcast, November 14, 2018.

94–95 *Developed by the Belgian software maker ImageLine*: Reed Jackson, "The Story of Fruity Loops," *Noisey*, December 11, 2015.

94–95 *Fruity Loops was downloaded as a demo, pirated, and in some cases actually purchased*: Alexander Iadarola, "13 Things All Fruity Loops Producers Know to Be True," *Fader*, October 31, 2014.

95–96 *Jenkins hears something new in how trap music deals with substance abuse*: Craig Jenkins, "Travis Scott Made This Year's Plushest Drug-Rap Album," *New York*, August 6, 2018.

95–96 *Scholar Kemi Adeyemi argues*: Kemi Adeyemi, "Straight Leanin': Sounding Black Life at the Intersection of Hip-hop and Big Pharma?" *Sounding Out!*, September 21, 2015. https://soundstudiesblog.com/2015/09/21/hip-hop-and-big-pharma/.

96   *Psychiatrists have used the song*: Akeem Sule and Becky Inkster, "Kendrick Lamar, Street Poet of Mental Health," *Lancet Psychiatry* 2, no. 6 (2015), 496–497.

96–97   *"Swimming Pools" has become a pro-drinking song*: Jessica Chassin, "How Did a Song with a Strong Anti-Drinking Message Turn into a Drinking Anthem?," *Huffington Post*, July 11, 2014.

Chapter 10

98   *I remember meeting Whitney*: "Beyoncé Remembers Whitney Houston," *Rolling Stone*, February 13, 2012. https://www. rollingstone.com/music/music-news/beyonce-remembers-whitney-houston-110709/.

99   *we form the strongest attachment to music we listen to as teenagers*: M. J. Stern, "Neural Nostalgia: Why Do We Love the Music We Heard as Teenagers?," *Slate*, August 12, 2014, https://slate.com/technology/2014/08/musical-nostalgia-the-psychology-and-neuroscience-for-song-preference-and-the-reminiscence-bump.html, accessed January 7, 2019.

102   *songwriter Dru Cutler uses the metaphor of an apartment building*: "How Beyoncé to the Beatles Modulate Your Emotions," *Switched On Pop* (podcast), September 9, 2016.

103–104 *Marc-Antoine Charpentier assigned subjective emotional qualities to each key*: James R. Anthony, *French Baroque Music from Beaujoyeulx to Rameau* (Portland, OR: Amadeus Press, 1997), 231.

103–104 *people with synesthesia associate keys with colors*: Mark Savage, "Charli XCX: Pop, Punk and Synaesthesia," *BBC*, December 12, 2013, https://www.bbc.com/news/entertainment-arts-25330600, accessed January 1, 2019.

Chapter 11

108–109 *we should think, instead, of identity as a 'production,'*: Stuart Hall, "Cultural Identity and Diaspora," in *Identity: Community, Culture, Difference*, ed. Jonathan Rutherford (London: Lawrence and Wishart, 1990), 222.

109   *dismissed "Oops!" as "hollow and fake,"*: Natalie Nicols, "Review: Britney Spears' 'Oops! . . . I Did It Again,'" *Los Angeles Times,* May 14, 2000.

109   *The fiercest invective*: Stephen Thompson, "Britney Spears: Oops . . . I Did it Again," *AV Club,* May 16, 2000.

110   *music journalist Ann Powers*: Ann Powers, "Women on the Verge: At the End of the '90s, a Few Artists Set the Stage for a New Era," *NPR Music,* July 31, 2018.

110   *writer Chuck Klosterman interviewed Spears in 2003*: Chuck Klosterman, *Chuck Klosterman IV: A Decade of Curious People and Dangerous Ideas* (New York: Simon and Schuster, 2006), 18.

110–111 *"artist-brands."*: Leslie Meier, *Popular Music as Promotion* (Cambridge, UK: Polity, 2017).

113–114 *Megan Lavengood dubs this maneuver "the cumulative chorus"*: Megan Lavengood, " 'Oops! . . . I Did It Again': Max Martin's Complement Chorus," presentation at the Society for Music Theory 38th Annual Meeting, St. Louis, MO, 2015.

115–116 *pop music has always been the "result of complex collaborative processes."*: Susan McClary, *Feminine Endings: Music, Gender, and Sexuality* (Minneapolis: University of Minnesota Press, 2002), 149.

116   *Berlin generated a series of "rules" for being an effective songwriter*: Charles Hamm, *Irving Berlin: Songs from the Melting Pot: The Formative Years* (New York: Oxford University Press, 1997), 3–18.

117   *Berlin, like Martin, was criticized for being a "hack"*: Dominic Symonds, *We'll Have Manhattan: The Early Work of Rodgers & Hart* (New York: Oxford University Press, 2015), 183.s

117   *"designed for public use."*:Simon Frith, "Pop Music," in *The Cambridge Companion to Pop and Rock,* ed. Simon Frith et al. (Cambridge: Cambridge University Press, 2001), 94.

Chapter 12

118–119 *"it's up to you how you want to interpret it."*:Alex Wagner, "Video+Interview: MIA, 'Jimmy,'" *Fader* video, August 7, 2007, https://www.thefader.com/2007/08/07/video-interview-mia-jimmy, accessed August 29, 2018.

119–120 *$70,000 price tag*:Simon Leo Brown, "Fairlight CMI Synthesiser, User by Stars like Michael Jackson, Added to Sounds of Australia Registry," *ABC Radio Melbourne*, November 17, 2015.

119–120 *"orchestral hit" sample*: Robert Fink, "The Story of ORCH5, or, the Classical Ghost in the Hip-Hop Machine," *Popular Music*, 24, no. 3, 2005, 339–356.

120 *Public Enemy assembled upward of 150 samples*: Mark Dery, "Public Enemy: Confrontation," *Keyboard* magazine, September 1990, 81–96.

120 *"I like to think of the MPC3000 as the piano or violin of our time."*:Estelle Caswell, "How This Legendary Hip-Hop Producer Humanized a Machine," *Vox* video, 10:23, December 6, 2017, https://www.vox.com/videos/2017/12/6/16742248/j-dilla-humanized-mpc3000, accessed January 5, 2019.

120–121 *"Thou shalt not steal."*: Biz Markie Grand Upright Music, Ltd. v. Warner Bros. Records Inc., 1991, 780 F. Supp. 182.

120–121 *this "law and order" line of argument*: Chuck Phillips, "Songwriter Wins Large Settlement in Rap Suit: Pop Music: Following a Court Ruling, Biz Markie and Warner Bros. Agree to Pay Gilbert O'Sullivan for Rapper's 'Sampling' of 'Alone Again (Naturally)'," *Los Angeles Times*, January 1, 1992.

120–121 *99 percent of drum samples were used without permission*: Sheila Rule, "Record Companies Are Challenging 'Sampling' in Rap," *New York Times*, April 21, 1992.

121–122 *Richard Prince*: "Cowboys," *Guggenheim Museums and Foundation*, https://www.guggenheim.org/arts-curriculum/topic/cowboys, accessed February 10, 2019.

122–123 *a single sample clearance routinely sells for $10,000*: Matthew Nelson, "Is Sampling Dying?" *Spin*, November 21, 2008.

122–123 *looking to monetize their newly minted intellectual property*: Kembrew McLeod, "How to Make a Documentary about Sampling—Legally," *Atlantic*, March, 31, 2010.

122–123 *Public Enemy would have lost $5 million on sample clearances*: McLeod, "How to Make a Documentary about Sampling—Legally."

123   *It's all replayed, by the way*: Eliot Van Buskirk, "Diplo Talks Sample of the Millennium, the Return of Fun and Other Musical Secrets," *Wired*, April 16, 2010.

125–126 *Diplo grabbed the gun samples from a more unlikely source*: Brendan Jay Sullivan, "La Bella Vie Worldwide De Diplo," *l'Optimum*, July 2013, https://medium.com/@MrBrendanJay/finally-found-out-where-diplo-got-the-gunshot-noises-for-paper-planes-f273d5ef5fa, accessed August 29, 2018.

126   *Sampling puts you in a very specific*: William Hutson and Jonathan Snipes, Interview with the authors, July 2018.

127   *A composition is not just notes*: Jonathan Snipes, Interview with the authors, July 2018.

Chapter 13

128   *James Murphy, leader of dance-pop outfit LCD Soundsystem*: David Renshaw, "LCD Soundsystem's James Murphy: 'Commercial Dance Music Makes Me Want to Vomit,'" *NME*, February 28, 2014, https://www.nme.com/news/music/lcd-soundsystem-2-28-1230998#Wz6qfjSRXXIT1vzC.99.

128–129 *Critic Ben Ratliff*: Ben Ratliff, *Every Song Ever: Twenty Ways to Listen in an Age of Musical Plenty* (New York: Farrar, Straus and Giroux, 2016), 7.

129–130 *As its composer has said*: Taige Jensen, Graham Roberts, Alicia Desantis, and Yuliya Parshina-Kottas, "Bieber, Diplo and Skrillex Make a Hit," *New York Times* video, 8:03, August 25, 2015, https://www.nytimes.com/video/arts/music/100000003872410/bieber-diplo-and-skrillex-make-a-hit.html.

133–134 *"virtual space."*: Eric Clarke, "Music Space and Subjectivity," in *Music, Sound and Space: Transformations of Public and Private Experience*, ed. Georgina Born (Cambridge: Cambridge University Press, 2013), 95.

134   *non-fans associate death metal with "tension, anger and fear,"*: William F. Thompson, Andrew M. Geeves, and Kirk N. Olsen, "Who Enjoys Listening to Violent Music and Why?" *Psychology of Popular Media Culture*, March 26, 2016, 16.

Chapter 14

137   *the new generation of reggaetón artists*: Eduardo Cepeda, "Urbano Reached Critical Mass in 2018. Now Can It Be Normalized?" *Pitchfork*, December 28, 2018.

137   *demographic diversity*: Julianne Escobedo Shepherd, "2017 Saw the 'Browning of America" Infiltrate Pop," *Slate*, December 25, 2017.

137–138   *offering danceable, off-kilter syncopation*: Wayne Marshall, "From Música Negra to Reggaeton Latino," in *Reggaeton*, ed. Raquel Z. Rivera et al. (Durham, NC: Duke University Press, 2009), 63.

139   *Axis progression*:Mark Richards, "Tonal Ambiguity in Popular Music's Axis Progressions," *Music Theory Online* 23, no. 3 (September 2017).

141–142   *"tonical neighborhoods"*:Philip Tagg, *Everyday Tonality II: Towards a Tonal Theory of What Most People Hear* (New York: Mass Media Music Scholars' Press, 2014–2018), 377.

142–143   *"why minor sad?"*:James Joyce, *Ulysses* (New York: Random House, 1961), 280.

143   *link between major chords and positive emotions*: Daniel Levitin, *This Is Your Brain on Music* (New York: Penguin, 2006), 38.

143–144   *in the late 2000s, only 42.5 percent were in a "happy" key*: E. Glenn Schellenberg and Christian von Scheve, "Emotional Cues in American Popular Music: Five Decades of the Top 40," *Psychology of Aesthetics, Creativity, and the Arts 2012* 6, no. 3 (August 2012), 196–203.

143–144   *mainstream news outlets wrung their hands*:Sarah Kliff, "Pop Music Keeps Getting Sadder and Sadder," *Washington Post*, May 31, 2012.

144   *Talking Heads frontman David Byrne has observed*: David Byrne, *How Music Works* (San Francisco: McSweeney's, 2012), 341.

144   *Leo Bloom returns to the question*: Joyce, *Ulysses*, 280.

144–145   *As scholar Wayne Marshall points out*: Marshall, "From Música Negra to Reggaeton Latino," 63.

Chapter 15

147–148   *When Martin first heard "Maps"*: Maura Johnston, "'Since U Been Gone': The Crossover Pop Needed, the Anthem Rock Deserved," *NPR*, August 30, 2018, https://www.npr.org/2018/08/30/643017969/american-anthem-since-u-been-gone-kelly-clarkson-pop-rock-crossover, accessed February 2, 2019.

149   *Indie music blogs*: Tom Hawking, "The Real-Life Stories behind 10 Famous Love Songs," *Flavorwire* blog, January 15, 2013, http://flavorwire.com/363625/the-real-life-stories-behind-10-famous-love-songs/7, accessed February 7, 2019.

Chapter 16

156–157   *Kofi Agawu*: Kofi V. Agawu, *Playing with Signs: A Semiotic Interpretation of Classic Music* (Princeton, NJ: Princeton University Press, 2014), 5.

158   *twang immediately conjures the South*: Jocelyn Neal, "The Twang Factor in Country Music," in *The Relentless Pursuit of Tone*, ed. Robert Fink, Melinda Latour, and Zachary Wallmark (New York: Oxford University Press, 2018), 49.

158   *"longing and loss"*: Joshua Guthman, *Strangers Below: Primitive Baptists and American Culture* (Chapel Hill: University of North Carolina Press, 2015), 120.

158–159   *the banjo continued to play a role in African American culture*: Tony Thomas, "Why African Americans Put the Banjo Down," in *Hidden in the Mix: The African American Presence in Country Music*, ed. Diane Pecknold (Durham, NC: Duke University Press, 2013).

159–160   *"scream for the unheard."*: Jeff Chang, *Can't Stop Won't Stop: A History of the Hip Hop Generation* (New York: St. Martin's Press, 2007), 328.

159–160   *an individual time signature*: William Jelani Cobb, *To the Break of Dawn: A Freestyle on the Hip Hop Aesthetic* (New York: New York University Press 2008), 87.

161–162   *segregated the diverse sounds of southern music*: Karl Hagstrom Miller, *Segregating Sound* (Durham, NC: Duke University Press, 2010).

161–162   *Burke's country songs were so popular with white audiences*: Peter Guralnick, *Sweet Soul Music: Rhythm and Blues and the Southern Dream of Freedom* (New York: Black Bay Books, 1999), 263.

162–163   *"I like every type of music . . . except country,"*: Nadine Hubbs, *Rednecks, Queers, and Country Music* (Berkeley: University of California Press, 2014), 50.

Index

For the benefit of digital users, indexed terms that span two pages (e.g., 52–53) may, on occasion, appear on only one of those pages.